The

Kate Millett

Prostitution Papers

A candid dialogue

Paladin

Granada Publishing Limited
Published in 1975 by Paladin Books
Frogmore, St Albans, Herts AL2 2NF

First published in the U.S.A. by Basic Books Inc 1971
Reprinted in 1973 by Avon Books
Copyright © Basic Books, Inc 1971
Copyright © Kate Millett 1973
Published by arrangement with the author
All rights reserved
This book originally appeared in
Women in a Sexist Society
Edited by Vivian Gornick and Barbara K. Moran
Made and printed in Great Britain by
Richard Clay (The Chaucer Press) Ltd
Bungay, Suffolk
Set in Monotype Ehrhardt

Contents

The Prostitution Papers

A candid dialogue

Introduction

The Prostitution Papers was written during what turned out to be the most hectic period of my existence – the summer of 1970. *Sexual Politics* was published in July and became a bestseller during August and September, exploding what had been a life of pleasant obscurity with the rocket of American 'success'. One of the most alienating aspects of the ordeal was that by the time the book was on the stands I had already ceased to be its author. That is, I had gone on to become a different kind of writer with a different style and different interests.

The Prostitution Papers played an important part in freeing me from the academic manner – distant, ironic, mandarin – with which I had begun as a writer. The galleys of *Sexual Politics* were put to bed by February. In the months that followed I became something of a full-time activist and organizer for the women's movement. In the spring of 1970 when the Cambodian war set off a national student strike and my own Experimental College at Columbia University disbanded so that its members could devote themselves to the peace effort, I was free to travel to a number of colleges in the North-east, the South, and the Midwest, doing all I could in the delightful role of outside agitator to bring young women into the strike as committed feminists.

With my friends in Columbia's women's liberation movement, I had begun to work out something of a feminist analysis of war as a social phenomenon and the militaristic mentality as a function of sex-role training. The time had come to put our theories to a test. How would our marginal young movement, with its oblique point of view, so vulnerable to the charge of non-participation – women are not drafted – how would it cope with the neo-militarism of the male Left, its macho obsession with violent methods? It was a high and glorious spring when much seemed possible. Hearing four thousand women's voices calling for Strike in the Smith College assembly hall, the word bounding from wall to wall, repeated over and over like a drumbeat in the centre of a whirlwind, I knew the satisfactions of an organizer.

However quiet, tangential, or imaginary my influence had been, I was living it all. Participation in politics was now a personal event. Not theory but practice: not the meeting of ten dedicated intellectuals in a New York apartment, but rallies in the rain before a college president's house, conclaves in buildings taken over by students, the terror of a police attack on the lawn at Columbia. And when I wrote of these things, fortuitously almost, on one occasion as a reporter for *Change Magazine* (because they paid my travel expenses), or another time as a contributor to the *Red Clay Reader* (because the editor was a friend and asked for something), I wrote as one *inside* the event. If I did not entirely abandon the irony in which I had been schooled, I no longer clung to that bleak pretence of objectivity routinely required of Ph.D. candidates. Ponderous sentences were whittled away to a natural length. Even to the sentence fragments in which we Americans actually think and speak. My language had to reflect the experience itself: colloquial, excited, immediate. Whether it was in the hurly-burly of strike work on campuses in the North-east, or in the painful nostalgia of revisiting a southern college where I had been desperately unhappy eleven years before – I was writing at last out of a direct emotional involvement. I began to write the way I talk and feel. In short, I was beginning to *write*.

The Prostitution Papers was something of a watershed in this process.* I was taught a deeper caring, another sound. In the earlier pieces, writing as a participant, I had jettisoned an academic style for one of personal reportage. It had been a relatively easy and liberating transition, exuberant and confirming. What happened with *The Prostitution Papers* was quite different. And at first it was agonizing, because through them I began to *listen* so that the experience of other women could pour over me. At moments I felt I was drowning in it.

Somewhere in my own contribution to the *Papers* I mention the fact that, after taping the interviews, I had to put them aside for a time before I was able to work on them as material from life, rather than life itself – so profoundly did they affect me, shake me, haunt me, overcome me. This absorption in the existences of other women, which I had undergone with *The Prostitution Papers* led to *Three Lives*, a documentary film which explores the biographies of three women, a film which I shot the same summer in the interval of taping the *Papers* and editing them. The filmed material also had to wait, to cool off as it were, for a few months before I felt sufficiently detached from my own overwhelming involvement with the human beings whose very lives had produced this footage, before I could even think of editing it.

I suspect there are a number of reasons for the somewhat traumatic effect which the material, in both cases, had upon me. First, the weight of its originality. For the actual life experienced by women has, until recently, been hidden from other women – inarticulate, unexpressed, foreign to the style and assumptions of our patriarchal culture. The eruption that takes place when it does surface is a common

* I refer here to the style of the four women's voices, rather than to the somewhat laboured manner of the preface, which appears when I read it now to have been composed as a justification for the straightforward talk of the women themselves.

event in consciousness-raising groups, where in a phenomenon which two anthropologists* have described as analogous both to the throes of religious conversion and the sudden cogency of pattern imposed upon insurgent peoples by social ideologies, a dramatic transformation takes place within individuals heretofore unable to define the insubstantial chaos of their lives. In consciousness raising a woman hears what had once been her own unique fears, grudges, perceptions, ambitions, and frustrations voiced by others. In consequence, she is suddenly assured that her experience is not, as she had imagined, aberrant and meaningless, but widely shared and eminently valid. But the other causes behind the strength of my reaction are both more personal and more general and they spring from my own peculiar almost hazardous tendency to identify with others, as well as from the wider moral implications which inevitably arise when one deals in others' lives. Entering into the sufferings of other women, exposing myself to them, no longer simply as a scholar or critic, but now as a writer or film-maker, I was exposing myself to them not only as an artist but as a woman, a woman each day more intensely concerned with the fate of all women.

It was impossible to discover the nightmare sense of entrapment which Mallory or Robin convey in the film, for example, or J's terrible despair in the *Papers* – without imaginatively becoming them and undergoing their pain as well. And this was exhausting. I also found that the knowledge of another's experience places vast moral responsibility upon you, since the very knowledge of another, if deep and authentic, constitutes great obligations.

How does one discharge such responsibility? Writing seemed merely the first step. But at least it was a start. If one could get some of the truth of the prostitute's experience into the open, in the forum of public discussion – if only to

* Esther Newton and Shirley Walton in an unpublished paper on women's consciousness-raising groups delivered before the Anthropological Association in New York City, 1971.

dispel the fetid air of sociological statistics or *Playboy* glamorization, or pornographic hype – then the fog of public apathy and misinformation might lift somewhat. Writing might spark discussion, it might arouse interest, it might direct attention towards the subject. It was also all that I could do on my own, as an individual. But it was not very much. It did not in itself change anything. And it was real change in the life of the prostitute which I wished to see come about, specifically any amelioration in her plight, the exploitation which encircles her on all sides, the degradation imposed by the pimp and the patron, the judgement of the law, the contempt of the public. A contempt that, despite bravado, becomes self-contempt. Through a dynamic familiar among all outcasts, the corrosive scorn directed toward the pariah from outside is interiorized by its victim, here the prostitute herself.

Change would of course involve specific legal reforms, decriminalization, also a redirection in police policy, but it would also imply more basic changes in attitude on the part of the public – that vast and elaborate process of re-educating people, which we have learned, as in the analogous situations of abortion or sodomy repeal, must precede legislative change. Essential to bring about such change in attitude is a dramatic shift in perspective in the world of 'straight' women, historically divided from the prostitute by their respectability. There must be a new climate of awareness, of trust and self-respect between women, a feeling of community. Most material of all, most difficult to hope for, meaningful change means change in the street. Some fundamental reorientation in the self-image of the prostitute which could affect her relationships with pimp, police, and patron. For of course the prostitute is the key figure – without her participation all discussion of change is condescending scholasticism.

Writing about prostitution might be a beginning, I thought, but unless others became involved, unless the women's movement or other coherent groups and organizations chose to focus on prostitution as an issue, the reality of the street world would in no way be affected by the publication of some mere essay in what turned out to be a large overpriced tome directed at an academic audience. I knew this and was discouraged at how little seemed possible, until the first feminist conference on prostitution was called in December 1971. I looked forward to the event with absurd optimism; at last things were beginning to happen. Other women cared, too. The thing might go forward, sped along with the strength of many women's energies. The results betrayed my Utopian naïveté. The conference was both an enlightenment and a disaster. The first day began sedately enough with information: excellent papers on theory, definitions, statistics, history, the convolutions of the law, its arbitrary enforcement (as, for example, in the case of 'wayward minors' or 'massage parlours'), and with proposals for reform. The afternoon was devoted to workshops where all hell broke loose – between the prostitute and the movement.

Because, against all likelihood, prostitutes did in fact attend the conference. Not many. Not perhaps the most representative. But a handful of women were there who were still in the life, rather than members of the movement who had turned a trick or nearly turned a trick under the pressures and exigencies of a past life. And these few came on like gang-busters. They had a great deal to say about the presumption of straight women who fancied they could debate, decide, or even discuss what was their situation and not ours. The first thing they could tell us – the message coming through a burst of understandable indignation – was that we were judgemental, meddlesome, and ignorant.

I had anticipated this confrontation, having experienced it on a much milder one-to-one basis before I was permitted to hear what I had learned about the life from my own informants over a year before when writing the *Papers*. I was also aware that outsiders do not organize. And that it is futile as well as pompous to play missionary.

And that if anything, ultimately, is to be done or said or decided about prostitution, prostitutes are the only legitimate persons to do it – whatever marginal or catalytic role the movement or movement writers like myself might play in beginning such a process.

Therefore the confused animosity of the prostitutes' attack, the uneasy guilt and muddled answers given back by movement women – both were predictable. After hours of heated and fuzzy argument we had drawn lines, stated positions, denounced each other – or rather the prostitutes denounced the movement, some of whose members would occasionally stop defending themselves long enough to listen or vie with each other for approval from their fellow prostitutes, who were enthralled to find themselves the centre of attention in a group of women they were free – even encouraged – to insult. An S and M trip. The spectre of sexual freedom, the real issue, was palpable in the room. Who knows most about sex? Who gets more? What is most? Who is cool? Money is fun. What's pride? What's prudery? Everyone was deeply ambivalent about everyone else: unconscious envy and resentment operated like steam engines – one felt them throb. We quarrelled and were reconciled, then quarrelled again – but at least we had come together. And in the interminable 'just let me finish my point' versus 'baby you don't know where it's at' that prolonged itself in doorways and staircases or over the post-mortem drinks in bars, we were at last becoming persons to each other. There was a gulf . . . but it was closing. It was all possible.

On the second day things exploded. An inadvertent masterpiece of tactless precipitance, the title of the day's programme was inscribed on leaflets for our benefit: 'Towards the Elimination of Prostitution'. The panel of experts included everyone but prostitutes. A few of them arrived late and after some hesitation were permitted to sit on the platform. As the last in turn to speak on the panel, I was delighted to turn over the discussion to the real experts. But it was already too late. Yesterday's ritual denunciations, gambits in a workshop foray, were now escalated into full-scale attacks before a large audience, a portion of it fresh and innocent, having missed the events of the day before. No structure or authority were recognized on the panel, whose members, new and old, fell out at once in tedious bickering.

The audience, outraged by having to wait its turn while being neither enlightened nor entertained, bewildered by the emotional and irrational squabbles of the panelists, revolted at last into long impatient lines before the microphones placed upon the floor for its benefit. When finally permitted to speak, the women, bottled up too long in the oppressive role of an audience, had also passed the point of coherence and gave themselves over to random tirades. Panelists left and were replaced by eager volunteers. A feast of unreason, I groaned to Alix Shulman as I watched powerless from the floor. Funny of course, if it weren't so awful. The fatuous but indefatigable peacemaker who also inhibits my soul wilted in despair. Private wars of wonderful acrimony broke out all over the room. No one listened. Everyone talked. No one made any sense.

Things rapidly degenerated into chaos. Prostitutes had gathered their still-nebulous rage against their own lives and summarily redirected it towards movement women who appeared to be quite as summarily 'eliminating' prostitution, the very means of their livelihood. Beyond the absurdly hypothetical threat posed by the term 'elimination', since the first step towards elimination was agreed by all the original panelists to be decriminalization – an obvious benefit to prostitutes who would no longer be arrested, fined, and imprisoned – beyond this was the far greater threat of adverse judgement by other women. For if large numbers of 'straight' women congregate to agree that there is an absolute benefit in the elimination of prostitution – what does this convey to the prostitute? That she is despised and rejected by her sister women. Never mind if this makes sense – it was there like an edict upon the heart. No denial, however vehement, carried any weight against this elemental conviction. All the sophistry of movement rhetoric – that we too are prostitutes, that all women are prostitutes, that marriage is prostitution, that prostitutes are oppressed and prostitution a form of slavery – all this is of no avail. Rhetoric, whose inflated metaphoric drift is the very stuff of radical politics, can not change the reality which the prostitute observes. The women on the panel and in the audience are not, in her literal sense, prostitutes at all. They are straights. Their marriages are not the same as her prostitution. She is not flattered by being labelled a slave. Even the prestigious title of 'most oppressed' has so little effect it could be rebutted with bravado – 'we make more money than you chicks!' Dialogue grows impossible. The hope of it noisily evaporates in screaming. And the adventitious element of personality makes its appearance: one of those who most persistently offered to represent prostitutes – a formidable actress whose grandiose neuroticism, however paradigmatic of the personal disorientation of an Uptown call girl, rendered her completely impervious to logic of any kind – took umbrage at everybody and everything. And took over. She ruled the occasion through an impressive hysteria which was equally effective upon her own contingent – increasingly silent, increasingly easy to manipulate – as it was upon her audience, cowed by her proclamation of authenticity. One watched in horrified fascination. A strange nervous woman with strange hair dyed some unlikely colour of grey, glamorous in a series of necklaces, ferocious in accusation, a Jesuit in argument, she grew and blossomed upon the stage, crowding out all other personalities in her euphoria of power. Mystic, an avatar, a force filling the banal ugliness of a school auditorium, she became The Prostitute, papal in her authority.

A chasm has opened. We are contestants, factions now, forever divided. The women of the movement, particularly the organizers of the conference who had believed they had acted in good faith, are put on the defensive. They become shrill. The contingent of prostitutes becomes shriller. Barriers rise. Positions become rigid. The accusation, so long buried in liberal goodwill or radical rhetoric – 'you're selling it, I could too but I won't' – was finally heard. Said out loud at last. The rejection and disapproval which the prostitutes have sensed from the beginning, and with the unerring instinct of the unconscious have directed all their energy towards exposing, is now present before us, a palpable force in the air. The prostitutes are justified at last. There is fighting now in earnest. Someone is struck, the act obscene, irreparable. Attempts at reconciliation are futile. Order and direction are out of the question in what is now an encounter group of more than five hundred people. The afternoon lies in shambles.

It was simply too early. Hope revived again when a remarkable young woman emerged, a freelance writer (the *Village Voice*, etc.) who worked and lived in a brothel. Here was the very combination of social and political savvy we needed, together with a generous and imaginative concern for her sisters in the life. Here was the organizer we had dreamed of. Further meetings were held, a group formed, a project outlined to provide legal and medical services to street women through a storefront. But as yet nothing occurs. And at present the group is disbanded, though it may yet be revived. Again it was too early. Again one has to conclude that the time was not yet ripe.

I am back at the beginning, left to pin my hopes on whatever may be accomplished through words. My own and the various, partial, often garbled reports on the conference which appeared in the *Village Voice*. However contentious and irrelevant these may have been – and they were often merely continuations of the quarrels which had destroyed the conference – the repeated blows of *Voice* reportage, like any other media notice, did provoke discussion and focus attention on prostitution. For a week or two people talked. Did street people hear? Do they read the *Voice*? Will they read this? And will they too grow impatient for their world to change? A writer can only hope.

New York City
May 1972

P.S. It may be that the West Coast will get it together before we do in the East. I have just heard of the agitation for decriminalization now being done by Margo St James in San Francisco and Jennifer James in Seattle. The best news of all is the project Margo St James is organizing out of Glyde Memorial Church in San Francisco. It is still early to predict successes, but the feeling of impotence lifts a bit. Things are looking up – it might just be possible that we could turn history around.

Sacramento, California
February 1973

Preface

It is my impression that emerging peoples have great difficulty with form. Baldwin's novels are very conventional. Edna St Vincent Millay and Elizabeth Barrett's poems have the sound of borrowed Keats or Shakespeare, dressed up to appear 'classical', and affecting the manners of the very best male poets. They are actually saying something different, something new. But they are saying it in an old way. Their derivative character makes it easy for the male academic establishment to denigrate and even overlook their substance. There are also rare eccentric figures, such as Gertrude Stein, saying new things in such novel ways that no one hears them at all. Then there is Virginia Woolf who combines both approaches in good measure. I never chose between the two, but if I had to, I would choose to admire Stein the more.

I should like to see the new movement give women in the arts a confidence in the value of their own culture (in the sense that females are a class with a subculture of its own) and a respect for its experience, together with the freedom, even the spontaneity, to express this in new ways, in new forms. I say this because I really love to see form become content. And if, indeed, we are saying something new, it does seem to me we ought to say it in new ways.

I have a strong feeling for the spoken language, for oral English. And women talk. Like the members of any repressed group, they are verbal persons, talking because they are permitted no other form of expression. When the prestigious intellectual and artistic media – be they traditional, such as poetry and philosophy, or contemporary, such as film or rock lyrics – are in the hands of those who govern, those out of power must settle for talk. One observes, for instance, a quite fantastic verbal ability in blacks. But women's talk has always been deliberately trivialized. And yet over the past five years, years I have spent in the women's movement, I have experienced a great change in such talk. There is a new cogency and direction, a clarity and rising consciousness in the speech of women now. I hear it in the conversation of women outside the movement as well as those within. And I attribute a good measure of this to the movement's acting as a cultural catalyst for numbers of women, many of whom are scarcely conscious, even unconscious, of its source.

What I have tried to capture here is the character of the English I heard spoken by four women and then recorded on tape. I was struck by the eloquence of what was said, and yet when I transcribed the words on to paper, the result was at first disappointing. Some of the wit of M's black and southern delivery had disappeared, gone with the tang of her voice. Liz's sincerity, her pain and concern, made an exact transcription digressive and repetitious. J's difficulty in speaking of things so painful that she had repressed them for years required that I speak often on her tapes, hoping to give her support, then later, edit myself out. My own transcripts read like the raving of an illiterate so I sometimes gave up on them and fell back into composition. As I grew more and more earnest about the project, I found the complexities of written English more appropriate in some places, a loose oral narrative more fitting in others. For all the voices it took a good deal of work to transform spoken to linear language, and I know I have not been successful in satisfying the demands of both. But I did learn a great deal about language: to respect the spoken word and to love its rhythms. Even to respect the tape recorder. For without this device to preserve the very sound of language, we should have no idea of how people *really* talk: their pauses, inflexions, emphases, unfinished sentences, short periods. All attempts to mimic spoken language seem terribly mannered, and one comes to respect Stein still more, and to admire how carefully she must have listened.

My options in this project – writing on prostitution – were to invent something myself, knowing nothing of the subject matter, or to eke it out of books, or else to begin the long and difficult process of finding women who could teach me. I took the latter course through a long and traumatic summer of intermittent work on the piece or of solemn anxiety during moments I was unable to work on it. Although I experienced for months a curious, defensive uneasiness over my inadequacy, never having been a prostitute as the term is generally understood, I did not finally succumb to the temptations of class guilt and delete my own voice or that of Liz Schneider, my collaborator, from the text. I decided instead on a four-cornered conversation encompassing very different persons, whose voices were instruments expressing their diverse experience. Without becoming fanciful, this reminded me of the quartet form. It is my hope that Liz and I contributed something by way of focus to balance the depth and validity of personal knowledge that M and J provided. Reading the piece in columns as one reads a score, I can hear J's voice, a first violin leading my own more subjective meander, then Liz's voice telling of her bitter experience in the courts, poignant as the viola, then M's resonant cello, vibrant, full.*

* In its original version *The Prostitution Papers* was printed as a quartet score in four columns across two pages (see Gornick and Moran's *Women in Sexist Society*, 1971, Basic Books). Space did not permit such an arrangement in this edition. In case the reader is curious as to what members of the quartet are doing now: J will finish a doctorate in psychology; Liz begins law school at New York University; after several years directing a drug rehabilitation centre, M has resigned her post to enter college. All royalties from this and other editions of *The Prostitution Papers* will be set aside for the work of assisting or organizing women in prostitution.

Seeing how the columns would read across the page, I winced to realize my own would commence with a remark on Baudelaire, M's with a reminiscence of a policeman accosting her as a prostitute and a junkie, then forcing his hand into her shirt. But these are in fact the directions from which we did approach the subject, and it would be pointless to hide this truth. Looking at the four columns on the page, Liz's and my own to one side, J's and M's to the other, the voices of two movement women merging with those of two women who have lived the prostitute's life and now either belong to the women's movement as does J, or are beginning to organize for it as is M, I could feel a certain gratification that, on paper at least (the reality is yet to come and will not be on paper but in the courts and on the streets), women are coming together from very different points of personal history or social origin. That is not, I hope, to disguise those differences in a fraudulent 'sister-hood'. Indeed, it is our very differences that make us unique and fascinating to each other as we join together in this movement, openly recognizing those differences – class, colour, religion, the varieties of our experience.

Loving someone is wanting to know them. In so far as we are able to learn and know of each other, we can acknow-ledge, and even in part assimilate into our imaginative life, the thousand differences that have always been used as wedges to drive us apart. So that the experience of all women everywhere becomes, in a sense, our communal property, a heritage we bestow upon each other, the knowledge of what it has meant to be female, a woman in this man's world.

J

The way that I got into it was like this. I was just broke and I had never liked to be in debt to anyone. I have a thing about it – being in debt. I've never liked to be financially dependent on anyone. I've always had this thing. What happened was I borrowed ten dollars from someone, and then I realized, after I borrowed it, that I couldn't pay it back. I had no way of knowing that I'd ever be able to pay it back – it was a man that I'd slept with too. So that's how I got into it. I just decided fuck it, man, I'm not going to be poor any more. I'd never been poor and I wasn't used to it. I was an undergraduate on a scholarship. My father was doing the worst he'd done in years. He couldn't afford to give me any money. They would have gone out of their way to give me money – my folks – especially if they'd known what I was doing to get it.

So I just went on the street. The thing that broke the ice had actually happened years before at a concert of Miles Davis. Davis was playing in a club, and someone outside wanted to take me. You know, asked me if I wanted to go in. And I knew that if I went in with him I'd have to sleep with him. But I figured it was worth it; I wanted to see Miles Davis. I had no feeling for this guy; I just wanted the ticket to get in there. I realized I'd whored – there was no way of denying the truth to myself. So when the time came a few years later and I was absolutely broke, I was ready.

I had talked to somebody and got a connection. I was living in an S.R.O.* over on Ninety-fifth Street, and there was this woman and one night she came down the hall and she said, 'I'm going out hustling tonight.' I couldn't have started by myself if I hadn't had a connection. And you make connections very fast if you're into it or want to get into it. She said she'd take me out and show me what to do, how to watch out for the cops, everything.

I didn't know I'd make really good money. But she told me to ask for fifteen dollars, 'take ten dollars if you have to, and if you're really broke, go down to seven dollars'. So I started off kinda slow, down Seventy-second Street, in high heels, and I must have looked inexperienced because no one made an offer. I walked until four in the morning and ended up in a coffee shop, exhausted. I'd walked all the way from Ninety-fifth Street down to Seventy-second, ending up in this coffee shop called The Laundry Chute. I don't know if anyone remembers it. This was pretty far back. But it was really nice. They had all these left-wing people, folk singers too, and I enjoyed that. Then I felt I ought to go back on the street and make some money. I'd got all dressed up and I had decided to do it. So I started to walk back. This guy came up in a grey car, and I got in. I was a little scared getting in the car. I didn't know what he would do. I think I brought him back to my place, and I think he offered me ten dollars. I might have asked for fifteen dollars. I don't remember how it went down. But he was very nice. I think he took my number, or something. I don't remember what we did either – I mean, in bed. I can't remember whether he wanted to pay my rent or not. I know there was another guy who definitely wanted to pay my rent.

I can never remember one job from another, but I do remember the first two. They all merge in a grey mass. A few of them stick out, like the one who gave me a bad

* Single room occupancy.

cheque. I wouldn't take cheques. I wasn't that stupid. But there are exceptions like this. Some guys always pay call girls in cheques and they're always good.

There are guys who come back time and time again because they can't afford to keep a call girl. They can only afford the ten or twenty dollars a week, so they come back because they can't afford anything else. I don't think they want all that, you know, a mistress. It becomes like a business relationship, time after time – a relationship like you might have with someone at the corner grocery.

There was one guy who wanted to pay me to beat him. It turns me on just to talk about it. I never thought I wanted to beat somebody, but when I did it, I felt I really liked it. I learned something that way – I learned that I really got pleasure from it. It wasn't sexy – it was not a sexual excitement at all. I guess I was getting back at all the men who'd done me wrong. I never get sexually excited in any relationship with a john. I've never made love with another woman. Now I guess I'm sort of neuter. I don't have sexual relationships now with anyone.

At that time, though, I'd have boy friends I really liked to sleep with. But as soon as somebody paid me any money, that changed the whole thing; made it the other thing. I see them as something else when they give me money. They might be the nicest people in the world, but it's something else, and you don't mix business with pleasure. I make a tremendous division between love and money. I don't get sexually turned on by somebody who gives me money. I didn't feel consciously degraded when somebody gave me money, but desire, affection, sex, feeling for the person, never entered into it.

And if you're on the street you have to take anybody who comes along, no matter what they look like – as long as they are reasonably clean. I didn't walk the street after that first time. I don't have to take just anybody. And if someone asks me to do something I don't want to do, I can refuse. I can refuse anybody because there were so many people.

New York is crawling with johns. And, what's very important, I wasn't dependent on any *one* man.

I was always scared to get into a car with somebody. I knew, second or third hand, of women who have been hurt by sadists, but I never got that kind. And I've seen women with marks and bruises that they got from their pimps. But I never knew anyone who was beaten up by a john. Of course it's different on the street. On the street you take anybody. On the street it's anything and anybody and, to a certain extent, whatever his sickness is, you're at his mercy. After that first time, I always worked through connections, but the first time it was a man in a car. This was an older man, with grey hair, and he was driving an old, grey car. A ten-dollar john. After that I didn't walk the streets any more because I was still waitressing and getting referrals from 80 Warren Street. Michael Harrington talks about 80 Warren Street in *The Other America*. It's an employment agency dealing in waiters and waitresses, cooks and things like that. I went down there one day to get a job. I was going to get a job before Saturday and this was a Friday afternoon. So there weren't any jobs and I was just hanging around. I ran into a guy there who was also looking for a job. He was trying to pick me up. It was a wild thing: I ended up going over to Brooklyn. He didn't want to buy me. I got scared he was a cop or something. He was pretty nice: a black guy. He wanted to set up a thing where he'd see me every week and go twice. His thing was going twice – for twelve fifty. And he wanted to pay my rent. Going twice – that means he screws me twice. It's a very bad deal because they take for ever going the second time. That going twice business, I got out of that.

I think the next connection I made was, I was riding on the bus. I got off at 102nd Street – somebody came up to me. I think I'd been in a bar trying to pick somebody up or something. It's very vague – all the sequences – but this guy, I took him home, and he gave me fifteen dollars. He was also black and said he could help me out. He introduced me to a lady who was in the life and who would show me around. This was the woman he was living with. He wasn't a pimp, no. He was a wonderful person. He was a numbers banker, and the woman he lived with was a whore, and they lived together. He was a really good guy. I don't see anything wrong with that. She had a boy friend whom she slept with because she wanted to. She eventually left him. I see him as a victim really. And this man really did a lot of favours and directed me to a lot of connections. He was my boy friend for a while. He always either gave me money or he got me connections. While he was getting me connections he always gave me money whenever I saw him. He wasn't flashy; not at all. But then in a way he was. He was such a good hustler, you know, and such a good con man. I never really knew him. But he was such fun to be with, such a good guy. He was an older guy – he was about forty-six – and he'd been in jail fourteen years, off and on, for everything. And it made him very difficult to know and very hard. I never really knew him. I never saw him without a façade. Soft he was, yes, but still I never knew him. Soft, in a special way.

There was one thing, though, and I think I've repressed it because I like to see him as a nice guy. It's not 'cause he's black he's a bastard. I don't have that white liberal hangup at all. Black people can be the biggest bastards in the world. Black people can be horrible people. I've seen more black sons-of-bitches than anything, and every pimp in the city's black. There are very few white pimps. And so it isn't his blackness that I was trying to protect in repressing what I'd remembered about him. It's that I like to see him as a nice guy. Now that I think of it – of course I don't know whether I'm paranoid or not – there was one funny thing that happened during the time I knew him. It was when I was in jail. That night I got busted, he wasn't around. And I was more worried about him than I was about me. He was busted, too; I was afraid he'd get prison. But what happened was, he didn't have to go away at all; he got off. And it could be that he might have turned me in and got off. Of course, I had no way of knowing because he was downtown and I was uptown. I was at Fourteenth Street then. And I didn't think of it until much later. I did wonder why I got busted, and I couldn't imagine who would have turned me in. But I didn't know anyone else who could have. Because someone had turned me in, and there were only two people who could have – this guy and a woman, and she'd got busted before me. Maybe her thing was to get off her sentence too, but this guy had been sure he was going to be sent away. And so I was so surprised when he wasn't.

He'd even been in for murder. I don't know if he'd ever killed anyone. I never knew. He never told me. But I assumed he'd done it. You know, he might have had good reason to do it. I never thought of it, but he might have killed me too, if he'd killed someone else. I never thought of it. He didn't seem especially violent; no more violent than most guys. I think maybe I romanticized his crimes a bit. I always imagined he committed murder in self-defence. Yet I never did ask him so I never did know.

He was in the numbers. I don't care though. There was one time, one thing he did, that did get to me, that was when he broke up a crap game and stole the money in the pot from a lot of poor black people playing. Of course, the numbers is a racket played off the black poor too. It isn't until now that I see how exploitative he was. But in those days I was always concerned with his being a nice guy.

*

When prostitutes put down other women, women like housewives, it's really only out of self-defence. Prostitutes feel that housewives are very moralistic people who even know that their husbands are cheating on them. While they're cheating on them they're seeing us. We're really not a threat to them; not at all. I wouldn't mind if I had a husband who went to see a whore. It wouldn't bother me. But then, if he had an affair with somebody, that would bother me – if he loved someone, if he got involved, then that would be a threat. The difference between being a prostitute and being a wife is the security a wife's got. But it's also the difference in having a lot of men versus having just one. If you have a lot of men – like if you have ten a day – then you're not dependent on any *one* of them. They can always be replaced; if one of them gives you trouble, you can just say 'fuck you'. But you can't do that if you're married and you can't do that if you're being kept. Of course, you can't depend on any john either. If the stock market falls, it's just like any other business. But that's the thing I wanted – never to be dependent. I spent the night with a john only once and I wouldn't even go out to dinner.

A lot of them wondered – they want to take you out to dinner, want to talk to you; they wanted to mimic the behaviour of lovers. Maybe that's what they want. Some of them really do want that – to be lovers. They fall in love with you. That's very hard to take. I never liked that. Because that was crossing the boundary – it wasn't business any more. And this was business; it wasn't love.

Johns are full of self-pity. They come on with this line about their wife doesn't understand them, and we follow right along with it. Or they turn us on to being good sports. And, you know, that made me feel great – that they'd say I was a good sport. They make you feel for a moment that you're somebody special, not a whore. When they would tell me I was special, I wanted to say, 'Baby, I'm just a plain whore. Forget that crap.' And the old line about 'How could a nice girl like you get into a business like this?' That's really said a lot. It's said a lot, especially by people who seem educated or middle class. And then sometimes they tell you that you aren't really a whore. I had a guy who I was seeing – about a month ago – I actually couldn't take it any longer. I saw him every week or every two weeks; he gave me a lot of money. Every time I saw him he gave me about sixty dollars, and I would see him for about an hour.

He was a very, very old guy – about sixty-seven. He was in love with me, and he would keep telling me, 'You're not a whore.' He was so hung up. Poor man. You have to feel sorry for someone who's that screwed up.

Johns go into this whole thing like, 'I want to leave her, but if I divorce her, she'll take all my money.' And they come on screaming and yelling about their alimony. I don't believe in alimony, but I certainly believe in child support. When you look into it, that's usually all they're paying, if that. And the wife, who's stuck taking care of the children, is doing him a service. In waiting on the child she's doing his work too because a child is something between two people.

You wouldn't have prostitution in a utopia. But you might still have it somewhere halfway between what we have now and a utopia. Prostitution might even, in a certain sense, be a reasonable service to be sold – sexual attention. But as it is now, I see it as a symptom, a symptom of the kind of sex we have here now. I think as long as you're going to have compulsive marriage and compulsive families, I think you're going to have prostitution. If I had a husband who wanted variety, it would be better if he had prostitutes than lovers. That's my hangup: I'm very possessive. I have this demanding possessiveness and insecurity. I wish I weren't so hung up on monogamy myself; I think it's idiocy. Monogamy and prostitution go together. There are lonely women all over New York, women sitting in bars, who would go with a guy, take him back to their place, make it with him, treat him well too – and be glad to do it. But instead men go to prostitutes on Seventh Avenue, Fifty-seventh Street, and Broadway, because there are no strings attached to a whore. And if you're married, that's a consideration. There isn't even that much chance that she'll be clean if she's from the street. But there are no strings attached.

I don't know why they go with girls from the street, unless they don't have connections. And there's always the chance of getting rolled. I really don't know why they go to the street. I think that it must be because there is nothing asked of them, even so far as spending the night. And then there are no games. You don't have to play seduction or anything. It's right on the table. And if they're worried about their masculinity, well, they're taking a chance with a girl if she's going for free. You don't know if she'll let you get laid or not. You might have to go through a lot of changes to get laid. And you might have to spend money and spend time. And a prostitute can't say, 'Well, I don't suck', whereas another woman might. She's got to do what he says or the deal is off. A pickup doesn't have to. You make the deal with her when you pick her up, you may do it without even speaking of it. But if she's chicken, well, you lose the whole thing – the time and effort. But with a whore, there's no risk, no gamble. Somehow you always pay for what you get, one way or another.

But what they're buying, in a way, is power. You're supposed to please them. They can tell you what to do, and you're supposed to please them, follow orders. Even in the case of masochists who like to follow orders themselves, you're still following *his* orders to give him orders. Prostitution not only puts down women, but it puts down sex – it really puts down sex. Often I really couldn't understand the customer, couldn't understand what he *got* out of this, because I really felt I was giving nothing. What he got was nothing. I could never see myself in his position, doing what he was doing. I would think it would be humiliating to buy a person, to *have* to offer somebody money. I felt the poor guy's gotta buy it; I felt sorry for him. He's really hard up. But then I remember he could be not so hard up as to have to buy, really; he wanted instead to have something so special you gotta buy it. I did not always see the gesture of buying someone as arrogance because I did not feel that controlled by the customer. I felt I was the boss because I could say no to the deal. I didn't want even the involvement of being a kept woman because then it's control again. When you're living with someone – when I was living with someone, that's when I really felt controlled. Then you can't refuse. People I've lived with, men I've lived with – I really felt that they had power because I couldn't say no to them. Because then I could lose them and, if I did, I would lose my whole life – lose my whole reason for living.

And with men I lived with, it wasn't just sex with which they controlled me. It was like pushing me around, giving me orders, unreasonable jealousy. There was one guy – I think of him all the time. When I think of a male chauvinist, I think of him. He's a black guy. He actually got me out of the business. He told me, 'Either you quit or I'll leave you,' so I quit and that's how I got out of it. It was a *man*, actually, who got me out of it. I got into it myself.

I felt freer of men as a prostitute than I would as a wife or a mistress or a beloved. Because he isn't there all the time – the john. Like for half an hour and that's all. And then someone else comes in. They really can't control you very much. You don't have the oppression that comes because you love the person and are so afraid of losing them. When you're a whore and somebody rejects you and says they want to see another girl, well, that's just part of the business. That's the reason he's coming to you in the first place – because he wants variety. It's much safer to do it for money, much safer.

You know, often it wasn't that a guy wanted to take over and invade my life so much. But that I would let them. I don't know if I'm still that way. I haven't tried lately. But in those days, I would let them do it. They didn't even have to want to. Like sometimes the guy might even resent it; he might want me to be more independent.

*

I don't think you can ever eliminate the economic factor motivating women to prostitution. Even a call girl could never make as much in a straight job as she could at prostitution. All prostitutes are in it for the money. With most uptown call girls, the choice is not between starvation and life, but it is a choice between $5,000 and $25,000 or between $10,000 and $50,000. That's a pretty big choice: a pretty big difference. You can say that they're in this business because of the difference of $40,000 a year. A businessman would say so. Businessmen do things because of the difference of $40,000 a year. Call girls do go into capitalism and think like capitalists. But you can't say, even of the call girl, that she has so many other ways to earn an adequate living. Even with an undergraduate degree, chances are that she couldn't do better than earn $5,000 or $6,000 a year, outside of prostitution. Because it's very *hard* for women to earn an adequate living and so we do not have much economic choice – even the call girl. And the minority woman on the street – the poor woman – she has no choice at all.

For white women you usually can't say that there's no choice but prostitution. There is. But the choice itself is a choice between working for somebody else and going into business for yourself. Going into business for yourself and hoping to make a lot of money. There's that choice. Prostitution on those terms is a kind of laissez-faire capitalism. But it's also slavery, psychologically. And it's also feudalism, where the protection of a pimp is offered in return for services. Unless you're starving so bad you literally have no choice – as some women do – the choice is between a lower-middle income and a really good one, lots of money. Lots of whores are on junk: it's expensive. A junkie has very little choice. For the junkie the only choice is getting off junk, a tough thing to do. Then too, a junkie off junk wouldn't be a junkie anymore. Prostitution is a kind of addiction too. It's an addiction to money. I felt that.

The worst part about prostitution is that you're obliged not to sell sex only, but your humanity. That's the worst part of it: that what you're selling is your human dignity. Not really so much in bed, but in accepting the agreement –

in becoming a bought person. When I really felt like a whore was when I had to talk to them, fucking up to them really while only talking. That's why I don't like to go out to dinner and why I don't like to spend the night. Because when they talk about 'niggers', you've just got to go 'uh-huh, uh-huh' and agree with them. That's what I really couldn't stand. It was that kind of thing. That's when I really felt I was kissing their ass – *more* than when I was literally kissing their ass. That's when I really felt that I was a whore. That's the most humiliating thing – having to agree with them all the time because you're bought.

That's why it's not as easy as just saying 'prostitution is selling a service'. That's why it's selling your soul and not selling a service. In business people sell their souls too, and that's why business destroys people – how would you feel about selling encyclopedias to poor people? But there's a special indignity in prostitution, as if sex were dirty and men can only enjoy it with someone *low*. It involves a type of contempt, a kind of disdain, and a kind of triumph over another human being. Guys who can't get it up with their wives can do it with whores. They have to pay for it. For some of them, *paying* for it is very important.

But a lot of them didn't make me feel degraded. Most of them didn't. If they had, I wouldn't have stayed. Some of them did – for example, the southerners. They were awful. And there's something about some men – the way they fuck – they lean on you and poke you with their bones. I'm sure they're not conscious of it. I found that so much more with southerners. They hurt me. And they've got to use all the *words* – all the words they can't say to their wives, covering you with the language of their shame. And their anger. That was another thing I didn't like either. When you're doing prostitution – if only in order to cope – you've got to have tremendous defences. You've just gotta turn off, somehow. Drugs or will power, you've got to cut yourself off.

I think that the conviction that females are dirty, that their genitals are dirty, really sticks to us. I think that's why I don't like men to go down on me. Because I think I'm dirty. I just don't like it because I think I must be dirty – and I think they're not. Maybe they clean themselves. A lot comes from this belief in our dirt – like I was douching all the time. Some of them like you to be dirty. One guy said to me, 'I would like it if you didn't douche for a week.' They want to go down on you and, another thing, they want you to come. That was another thing that I didn't like. Here I go, thinking about all the things I don't like. And now I'm really getting into it. I know I didn't like it and I don't want to get into it again. One of the worst things about it was the faking. You had to fake orgasm. They expect it because that proves their masculinity. That's one of the worst things about it. That's really being a whore, being so dishonest. I don't know how they believe it – johns. Some of the ones I've had were even bachelors – good-looking guys with a lot of money, eligible young men. Very good-looking with a lot of money, didn't want to marry, wanted to go to whores. They had a tremendous fear of getting involved because that's giving something.

*

When I wanted to get out of it, one of the things which made it very difficult was that I wanted to get married. This was one of the reasons I got out of it – I thought I was going to get married. And you can't go on if you want to get married, unless there's a pimp who wants to marry you and put you to work. I think the worst thing about prostitution was the way it spoiled my relationship with men. It's very hard to be common property like that, hard to find a man who'll put up with it. They either want you to quit or they want to take all your money, and there're very few men who don't fall into either one of those categories. Most of the ones I'd like would want me to quit. The other ones want my money. The only exceptions I've been able to find are gangsters. And the guys who want you to quit, they want you to be true, like they feel you're cheating if you're whoring. Very few men will understand that when a woman screws for money, she has no involvement at all. Yet *they* can just go out and get laid and feel no involvement. But they don't understand how you can do it for money and feel nothing. They think you're cheating and they can't take that. And the guy who wants you to quit: he's seeing you as property; he's changing you, from like currency, which passes from hand to hand, to something like real estate. *Real* property. There's an *owning* thing about wanting you to quit, especially if the guy is poor.

And I don't want to be kept. I don't care how much I love somebody, I don't want to be kept. Because anyone who keeps me has power over me. To ask someone for money to buy something, that would be so demeaning. I couldn't do that. I'll tell you what it is with the money and not wanting to be kept. If I loved someone and were dependent emotionally, then to be economically dependent too would be terrible. At least let me be financially independent because I'm so dependent emotionally. I have a tremendous thing about this; I had it with my parents too. I'm getting a little better about it with them. Because I feel so helplessly at someone's mercy.

Yet dating, for example, I found so much more humiliating. It's the same thing as prostitution – they're buying you, but they're doing it indirectly. And we're all pretending that this isn't happening. You see I can't pretend. Because I know what it's about; that's why I can't do it.

Men think that sex once is sex always, on demand. If you go out with them and make it, you're their thing. Maybe you haven't got laid in six months, but they don't consider that. It's a terrible disappointment. I feel like sleeping with somebody sometime. Then he turns out to be a real son of a bitch – like he'll introduce me to his friends. His friends I don't feel like sleeping with; I just want to say 'fuck off'.

But the friend is so sure he's going to get laid because you slept with his pal – as if they felt they could *loan* us or 'fix us up'. And if you don't put out, they call you a lesbian or else they'll say, 'Are you prejudiced because I'm black?' You're getting cornered all the time. But when you whore, at least you're getting something back – you're getting cash. So in a sense whoring is less oppressive. And with the cash you can do anything that you want to. Cash – you can get it from a southern racist and give it to the Black Panthers; you can do what you want to with it. With the dinner and the date, what can you do? Just get fat. And they force you to eat a lot or drink too much so they can lay you.

I would so much rather turn a trick with somebody than go out on a date. Turning a trick is not anxiety-producing. But going out on a date, I just freak out. Of course, on a date you may kid yourself that it's your personality they like. But when you're whoring, it's sometimes your personality they like too. There's one guy who comes to the studio regularly, he does other things with other people, but he gives me ten dollars just to talk to me. For shrinking too, you get ten dollars while they talk. And that's why I think I'm going into it. When I was in therapy I saw such parallels between the two things – prostitution and psychiatry – kinds of therapy. And then all the money they make. Like, I thought, here's a way I can legitimately do all this. I felt always that my analyst was doing the same thing I'd been doing, but respectably.

Psychology today is really into keeping us in our little cages, but I still hope that that isn't all there is to it. I can't even be that sure about my analysts. My first analyst I'm not too sure of; nor my second. But the second did a lot for me. After all, I was in prostitution before I got into therapy. In fact, I couldn't afford analysis until I was a prostitute. And therapy is what got me back into school, into graduate school, and out of prostitution. And the parallel between therapy and prostitution is a parallel that I often draw even to the analyst. It was freaky, comical. I certainly hope he didn't do less work than I did – because I want to get *my* money's worth. I want to *get* something for my money, and I know those johns didn't. The analyst sells a service which does not degrade him, but makes him distinguished and respected.

When I try to think of prostitution as selling a service, I have to remember that most people don't sell services to others. They just trounce all over them and call it competition. Then when I think, how did the john get the money he pays me? By exploiting another woman – a secretary, or someone like that, a wife. The boss is likely to sleep with his secretary on the side. She's doing it for nothing and that's really horrible. Secretaries and women in sweat shops – places like that – are put in the position where they feel that if they don't put out, they'll lose their job.

I don't feel that I'm a whore now, but the social stigma attached to prostitution is a very powerful thing. It makes a kind of total state out of prostitution so that the whore is always a whore. It's as if – you did it once, you become it. This makes it very easy for people to get locked into it. It's very hard to get married; then too, most of the people who do it are not that well educated, not that many of them could do any other job. You get locked into it simply because you get hooked on luxuries. You can get hooked on consumerism, or even just on living decently. You can get hooked on a certain kind of freedom, where you can go where you want to without being beholden to someone who supports you. For me prostitution didn't even offer good hours 'cause I had this work hangup. I worked about twenty-four hours a day – I was into making so much money – obsessive about it. I can also see how people could be trapped in it because it's so hard for them literally, objectively, so difficult to do anything else, let alone to do as well economically.

But however underpaid a woman factory worker or a typist may be, she still has something the whore doesn't have. Even I wanted to have a legitimate front. I had to do something else too. Lots of call girls have done secretarial work from time to time. I don't put women down who have straight jobs. I wanted a straight job more than anything and I'm going into a straight job. I'm not going to make any more money. I may even, as an intern, make less than the average secretary and a great deal less than I made when I was in the life. Yet I'm looking forward to it. Because you are selling a *lot* when you are being a whore. You're giving up a lot. One thing you're giving up is a chance to have a normal relationship with a man.

As a prostitute you're alienated, isolated even, not only from yourself but from the rest of society because you can't talk to people about it. And when I was doing it, I only had friends that I could tell about it, people in the life. For the power of straight society to oppress prostitutes – for that to – disappear – prostitution has to be legalized. Right now you can't even tell people because of the law. And the cops are very scary, very hard to spot. Ugliest bastards in the world driving around in old Plymouths. They are frightening because they can pick you up. If you were able to tell people, that that's what you do, if it weren't assumed that that's what you're always going to do, you would be able to leave it and do something else. Imprisoned in it – you shouldn't be imprisoned in it all the rest of your life. Having done it now prevents you from doing anything else in the future. You're vulnerable if you quit – I am myself – in regard to my fellowship. I probably will be even after I finish my degree and internship. Yet you ought to be able to go straight whenever you want to.

Funny – that expression, 'go straight' – same expression that's used for gay people. I wonder what's the opposite of going straight. Crooked? I wonder what is synonymous with going straight – being perfect, I guess. It's funny that both those worlds should use that expression. The underworld too – 'going straight'. All three groups are outsiders.

If you tell me that being in the life is beating yourself up psychologically, I can't help but resent that. Because psychologically I've suffered so much more in other situations, been humiliated much more in other situations. I think the money had a lot to do with my feeling freer. I didn't feel I was taking nearly so much shit when I was in the life as I do now that I am a teaching assistant. As a teaching assistant I am really put down and I don't make nearly as much money. True, it carries a certain social status that's a lot higher than that of a prostitute, but you pay for it, you really pay for it. I worked long hours for little money and I took shit. I was in tears so much more in graduate school, infuriated and sick. I didn't get an ulcer when I was a prostitute. That happened when I was in graduate school.

And I'll tell you, I have not cried nearly as much being a prostitute as I have being a student. It's different somehow. When I was a prostitute it wasn't *me* somehow. I didn't get put down in the same way. I didn't feel it as much. You just don't get that put down in the same way. Maybe because you're down so far, you just can't get put down any further when you're a prostitute. The street is the street and you expect nothing from it. The academic world I did expect something from. You're always defensive with johns. You never invest your ego with them. But I did with the university. After all, this was going to be my profession. The university was going to be my way out from the street – from being a prostitute. What a disappointment. School just doesn't have to be that way – they just don't have to humiliate you that way. They should just treat you with respect, for God's sake. All I want is respect, for God's sake. I don't want unconditional love, just respect.

As for me, I feel better about being a prostitute than being married to somebody I can't stand and being locked into that. If I were the slave of a pimp and getting beat up all the time, I would see that not as prostitution but as another kind of marriage. It's very hard to find a prostitute who hasn't got a pimp, and so I'm not really representative of prostitutes. I not only didn't have a pimp, but my education also makes me unrepresentative. But I'm not so different either – consider the devotion I had to whoever my lover was. And the dependence I had is the same devotion that the average whore has to a pimp except I wouldn't let him take any money or beat me. With me it's got to be more subtle – but it's the same goddam thing.

I'm terribly messed up as far as sex is concerned – that's why I could become a prostitute. I've always been messed up as far as sex is concerned. Now I don't relate to men at all. It's easy to go along with what most people say about prostitution 'cause they read it all in a book. But I'm not going to say it's true unless I feel it. And I do hate prostitution – I do hate it. That's why I'm not doing it now. I spent all these years in school just to get out of it. If I liked it I'd be there now. At the time I was so numb that I felt nothing. I hate it now because now I feel. I just can't stand it now when people touch me. I just can't stand being put there. Here I've had all these years of education and I should still have to do this and I'm still expected to put out. And now it's for a lousy dinner. Even with my Ph.D. Now I hate it but I won't project about how I felt about it then or failed to feel. I did, I must have hated it then. But I wasn't aware of it or I couldn't admit it. I think I'm getting better now, now that I realize that I hated it so much. But now I'm getting so I hate men. I'm getting so that I avoid men. What I am is I'm becoming aware of how much I always hated it. And I know now how it has ruined all my relationships with men. We are so afraid to say that we hate men. So the prostitute finds a pimp and says this is the one man I can love. And he treats her like dirt. I've become aware of hating men, and I've been afraid to say it for a long time. I'm becoming aware of how the whole experience just freaked me out. They put you down for what they have made of you. I learned this lesson too well – first when I got put down in school, then you get put down for having done prostitution so you learn the lesson all over again. Say you come out and do it honestly and sell yourself for money. And then you're put down for that.

When I became a prostitute I didn't feel my will being broken. To become a prostitute was just the easiest thing in the world – I was ready for it. Because sex had never meant much to me at all. So I could make money with it; might as well use it for that. Most of the time it just didn't mean anything at all: I guess that's what made me ready. And that didn't change when I was in the life. I felt nothing, a lack of feeling in sex. Except with special people. And with the special people there was this terrible emotional dependency which is really the way a prostitute is – although she doesn't feel anything when she's out hustling. And they're just hung up and depend on their pimp – so I was into that. That I could screw all kinds of guys and not care. Screw. Maybe get screwed by is the right word.

Long before I got into prostitution I would go to bed with guys, because I thought I owed it to them, because I'd 'led them on' or some bullshit. I let them con me into that. And when that happens you just lay back and say 'Okay, I got myself into this. Go ahead, I don't care – do it. Go ahead, do your thing.' Passive. Even being passive is a way of resisting. It says, yes, you can have my body, but you won't get me excited. Neither angry nor sexually excited. The scary thing about it is the way I put myself out, asleep inside. Now if you're actually making love to a guy you get tired, use up energy. But if you're passive as I was, you use up little, you suppress it all. When I was a whore I never got tired, never exerted myself.

I could anaesthetize myself so that I didn't suffer that much. But a lot of whores can't. They're really in conflict all the time. I had a friend like that become a junkie. She wouldn't *be* a whore. She refused. But then she became an addict. She had an old man who put her out on the street. And she hated it. If I'd been like that I would have gotten myself out of poverty some other way. It was because it

wasn't painful that I could do it. I think I couldn't take it
now.

I didn't have a bad life in prostitution. Primarily, I
didn't have a pimp. To organize prostitutes the hardest
thing about it will be to get around the pimp. You're gonna
have the pimp down on you; after all, his livelihood and his
interests are threatened. I saw some pimps today – two
black guys with Texas plates – I'll say they had guts. There
they were with those Texas plates on a 1970 Cadillac with a
blue-flowered convertible top. Man, those guys had class.
Ever seen a Cadillac with a flowered top? Nothing but a
pimp or possibly a rock 'n' roll star would ever sport that –
but they're usually pimps on the side or whores of one kind
or another before they got to be stars.

Pimps really do nothing. They don't get you dates. They
provide no service at all and do nothing at all all day. They
gamble, they drink, they beat you up. They ride around in
them Cadillacs. They look pretty. They stink from perfume.
Pimps don't do a damn thing for you. They spend all your
money. That's what they do for you. They'll bail you out of
jail only 'cause you're their money. But you can bail yourself out of jail and you can keep your own money. You don't
need a pimp.

Most prostitutes do have pimps. I can understand where
they're at. Because I was into the same thing, the same type
of dependency. I just didn't give the pimps my money. It's
this love thing – the dependency. For most prostitutes the
pimp fulfills the romantic ideal of true love. For me it was
different – a poor scroungy student was my true love. And
I wanted to give him my money – I really wanted to. But
he wouldn't take it. True, I was a student too and just as
scroungy. But I didn't see myself in the same romantic light
I saw him in. He was a leader, a revolutionary. He wouldn't
take my money. I tried to force it on him but he wouldn't
take it. I was his suffering proletariat, his Mary Magdalene.
Then he went off and married someone else. He married a
good girl. I felt he had a mind and was important: the

45

idealist, the rebel. He was always better than me. I felt lucky to know a great fellow like that. Yes, and the dangers and temptations of the leadership trip: I saw them. Most of these guys take care of themselves. A few years after college they're in a law firm or they're out hustling like Jerry Rubin. Everybody hustles. They hustle the revolution. They prostitute it. Off on their ego trip.

I'm not free of this guy yet. I was still in love with him last summer. And I'm not sure I wouldn't go to bed with him again if he came to New York – I can't say for sure that I'd be able to tell him to fuck off. I did say no to him last fall. He wanted to come to New York and I said no. At least as a prostitute you can say, 'Yes but – yes but I want fifteen dollars.' If you're a good chick all you can say is yes. One thing I did accomplish: he wanted me to go back with him and I refused. That's probably why we're not together now. He wasn't going to stay here with me – that hadn't occurred to him as an option.

I think I only once had a john who was a college boy, a student like myself. But once I told a professor I was doing prostitution. I told him half jokingly. And he set up a bachelor party for me. He was going to do it, anyway, and thought he'd hire someone he knew. He wasn't actually my teacher – I wasn't in his course. He could have said no. You do occasionally meet guys who say no. But that's very rare, because it's the men who initiate it. I can't put this guy down especially, just 'cause he's a professor. All jobs are alike really – a john's a john. It wasn't like he was corrupting me or something. This was my business. If he'd come on moralistic with me I would have really hated him. If he started giving me that crap I would have been mad. I lead my own life. I'm not going to let any john tell me. I may have hated prostitution but I had the *right* to do it. I don't like people telling me not to do it. Gets me mad, when they tell me not to do it – that I'm too good for it and so on and so forth. I feel that's a 'superior' kind of attitude, morally superior. I get very tired of the people with that 'healthy' nonsense – the argument that prostitution's not psychologically healthy. They have a double standard about prostitution, you know. I could be doing all kinds of self-destructive things and they wouldn't mind. They wouldn't criticize me for self-destructiveness if I were just as compliant or masochistic outside of prostitution, as a girl friend or wife. I could be doing much worse things to myself, and they would approve. When they tell me, 'You shouldn't do it, it's bad for you,' I hear, 'You shouldn't do it, it's bad.' And I hear them saying, 'I'm superior, what a wonderful person I am to speak to you and lift you up, you fallen woman.'

I like to believe I have some kind of free choice. Some choice in my life. That I chose a lesser evil. I wanted to do it. And somehow I want that to be respected. I *wanted* to do that. Somehow their pity deprives me of my freedom of choice. I don't want to be saved; saved by the Christians or saved by the shrink. Whatever the rationale is, it's the same: condescending, patronizing. Something in me just resents this moralism, their uplifting. I'd like so much to have the illusion that I had some freedom of choice. Maybe it's just an illusion, but I need to think I had some freedom. Yet then I realize how much was determined in the way I got into prostitution, how determined my life had been, how fucked over I was to have no confidence in myself. But I had to get myself out of it somehow. So I believed I'd chosen it. What's most terrifying is to look back, to realize what I went through and that I endured it.

When I look back on prostitution, I have so much ambivalence. I'm not even sure how I feel about it. It's not all negative. In remembering it, I was so afraid to come off with the ready answers the shrink had demanded. It's really more complex. So there was much that I denied, because it was only too painful to remember. Also I had seen how much conformity there was in the therapist's way of regarding it so I resisted that kind of pat answer. I denied at first what I can remember feeling – how in the beginning I just hated the men, just wanted them to stop touching me. To just get away.

K

Prostitution is something I've had on my mind all this year. Last fall I did some reading on it with my students in the experimental college, first defining prostitutes as a social group, then studying their collective behaviour. When the American Philosophical Association asked me to talk at their Western Meeting this spring, I offered to discuss prostitution, homosexuality and abortion as three instances where the law infringes upon sexual freedom. Whereupon their enthusiasm waned and the invitation seemed somehow to evaporate. Then Vivian asked me to do something for this book. I chose to write on prostitution, and I chose it with some determination.

Everything I've read on prostitution, even the way it is discussed, pisses me off: the statistical approach of sociological texts, the cheerful rationalizations of popular accounts, the romanticized versions of literature. One is slowly forced to realize that for centuries a tremendous moral and sociological confusion has surrounded the entire issue, a phenomenon one can account for only by considering the monumental sexual repression within our culture, and its steady inability, after having created both the prostitute and her plight, to recognize her as human in any meaningful sense at all. The smug stupidity with which people are accustomed to discuss the subject is fairly outrageous: the victim, the prostitute, rather than the institution that victimizes her, is condemned. Prostitution is regarded as humorous, inevitable, or convenient, the prostitute is derided, castigated, or pharisaically informed that her situation is of her own choosing and 'her own fault'. As the causes of female prostitution lie in the economic position of women, together with the psychological damage inflicted upon them through the system of sex-role conditioning in patriarchal society, this conventional satisfaction with the prostitute's fate is not only unjust, but simplistic.

Lately, apologists for that custom of trafficking in persons which we call prostitution have overhauled the tired machinery of the double standard, and hailed this enslavement of women as 'sexual freedom'. This is to subvert the promise of sexual liberation into a tawdry licence to exploit women further through state brothels complete with a medical assurance that the males who patronize them do so without risk. This is to foster and acknowledge the prostitution of women as a privilege of the state. It is even more vicious than the present system, general throughout the United States, of harassing and prosecuting the prostitute with summonses, fines, and imprisonment, punishing in the female an offence society does not think to punish in the male. (Male prostitutes sell themselves to other males and are a parallel case here, not a contradiction.)

It is a further irony that our legal ethic prosecutes those who are forced (economically or psychologically) to offer themselves for sale as objects, but condones the act of buying persons as objects. Yet the system of exploited labour called voluntary servitude, practised under the indentured-servant code of colonial America and clearly analogous to prostitution, would never be permitted today and was outlawed even before the abolition of Negro slavery. Rather than state regulation or repression of prostitution, the course of justice would appear to lie in another direction: namely, in removing prostitution from the criminal code altogether. Decriminalization would in no way increase the incidence or availability of female prostitution, but it would frustrate the exploitation of prostitutes by the two classes of men who are their chief predators: pimps and police. The latter function in the same manner as pimps, since the fat earnings of members of the vice squad are acquired through methods of coercive protection. One defines a pimp as a male who lives on the earnings of a prostitute. Since the prostitute is a lucrative source of police graft, forced to endure either extortion or arrest, government has a vested interest in prostitution's illegality, rivalled only by those states that in 'regulating' (e.g. institutionalizing) prostitution, make it a state monopoly. Oddly enough, the other chief opponent of the decriminalization of prostitution is not organized religion, but powerful hotel interests, who see the prostitute's patronage as insufficiently lucrative to outweigh her possible threat to the public image of the more expensive hotels affluent enough to dispense with her custom.

*

To educated women the prostitute is probably only familiar through literature. The woman as whore is a literary archetype of greater frequency than the actual prostitute population would ever warrant, a version of female existence insisted upon by the men who create our high culture. It is difficult not to find the literary man's impressions of prostitution particularly annoying. Baudelaire and his zest for 'evil' come to mind. The glorification of the golden-hearted whore is a cheap and easy stunt: in identifying with her the poet feeds his self-pity; in condescending to her he congratulates himself on his humanity, his special insight in perceiving the suffering Magdalene in a mere woman of the people, a creature of the street. And in sugaring her situation, or clothing it in sentiment, he perpetuates it as surely as French tourism does. There is a perfection in all this: the liberal fellow has found moral credit through patronage ... and he is still fucking the whore while congratulating himself on noticing her misery.

*

But I am a woman, so there are more personal motives behind my interest in prostitution. I remember the tenor of the first conversations I had with Liz Schneider on the subject. We both felt we had no real right even to speak. We had been to college; we had never sold for cash. Not bound by the same economic iron maiden many prostitutes are, nor even well-informed on the call girl's life, we felt presumptuous as well as ignorant. And yet, we argued, here was a great informational blank since one does not hear honest accounts from the subjects themselves, but suborned nonsense invented either *by* men or *for* their satisfaction (see the glowing accounts of the party girls found in men's magazines). Nearly all other information on the subject is limited to male sources. Someone, we agreed, must begin getting some truth out, if only because people have been misinformed so long and the misrepresentation continues.

I knew, or I thought I knew, how difficult it would be to find informants, to acquire and deserve their trust, to forge past the prostitute's habitual defences – the product of her social and legal persecution. But I underestimated the difficulties, just as I never foresaw the depth of my eventual involvement, my growing feeling of commitment to (and ultimately, identification with) a group of women whom I came to know through friendship with a few of them. So wronged, so utterly exploited – it made me furious. Or afraid. Because like all women, I know the prostitute exists as an object lesson to the rest of us. Like the squaw in the Westerns, docile and on foot behind her master, an example even if purely fictitious, the whore is there to show the rest of us how lucky we are, how favoured of our lords, how much worse it could go for us.

Staying up all night talking with J, chilly with fatigue, 'though it was summer, making a new pot of coffee to keep us awake, or sitting in M's apartment in the early evening, the broad leaves of a courtyard tree filling the white room with a cool green serenity – we were women talking about things that physically happened to these two women, yet in a sense, psychically happen to all of us. For there are more immediate reasons behind any woman's interest in prostitution, that come to mind more quickly than mere academic interest. Or even a woman's liberation version of prostitution, highly analytical, drenched in rhetoric and superior theoretical insight. Or a Marxist table of wage scales balancing the oldest profession with the less remunerative categories of woman's work. There are better and more homely reasons why all women are conscious, or paradoxically, refuse to be conscious, of prostitution.

A woman does not really need all that much imagination to have some insight into the prostitute's experience. I found a recess in my mind, a 'closet' I call it, which, probably like most of us, I had always dimly perceived yet hesitated to approach, a fantasy mesmerizing me for half a lifetime, the fifteen or twenty years since adolescence. It occurs to me to wonder if the night riders hold any of this hypnotized value for blacks. Or would it be the New Orleans Market? In any case, what is it like to stand on Broadway tonight . . . ? Perhaps the rest of us are merely deceiving ourselves – it is ultimately an experience we all share. But diluted. I think many of us, maybe all of us, are really selling and not knowing we're doing it. The question lies then in who among us *could* stand, or will *have* to stand, on Broadway tonight.

*

The watered-down character of our own prostitution occurred to me and to Liz the moment we remembered dates and dinners. I kept thinking back to a time when I first got my Bowery studio. The girl I lived with then had split and I was very alone. I was broke too, living on the forty dollars a month my mother sent me out of what she earned selling life insurance to people who didn't want it. The loft was as cold as hell. I was sick all the time. Bronchitis. The only heat was a little pot-bellied stove; used to sleep with the damned dog to keep warm. And there was a young doctor chasing me around for a few months. I suppose there's some popular masculine belief that women artists are something special, you know, 'liberated women'. An interesting or an easy lay. This Brooks Brothers suit, Doctor John, began giving me a big rush. He took me out to dinner for a couple of weeks running. Then I began to think I had to make it with him. What was I putting out? He was putting out dinner. I needed the dinners, but I really could have used the cash. Sixty, maybe one hundred dollars; a whole month's rent was only fifty. John wouldn't buy sculpture. And he didn't seem to find my art interesting, still less to care about my soul. Would I have taken advantage of J's 'connection' into prostitution if I'd had it then? Or did the garbage I made out of plaster in those days give me so much purpose and satisfaction I could pass up cash money? So I got five or six steak dinners in four weeks, held aloof from the doggie bag, and got laid for free.

*

Then I thought of the time when I really did plan a sale. It was when I had just finished college. I was going to Oxford, the rich relatives having swooped in at this juncture, offering the money to send me. I was not going alone, but with someone I liked, loved actually. A woman. The relatives didn't take to this at all . . . true . . . a *pervert* in the family. They held a tribal council just to discuss my crime, aunts and uncles flying in from all parts. The upshot was that I had to renounce my friend or give up Oxford. Didn't do either: I lied to them and went to Oxford with her. But before she could go, we had to find the money. I worked in a factory all summer and there still wasn't enough saved up. My friend was a graduate student with a place in the ghetto near the university. We lived in a rooming house, ate the food she brought home from waiting on tables, and kept a Dalmatian who turned out to be deaf and capable of resisting our every effort at house training. Mother broke out in Sophie Portnoy tears upon seeing the place. It was the happiest summer of my life.

But by summer's end there still wasn't enough money. So I got a brilliant idea. I would sell myself for no less than a fortune and make us rich quick. I was younger than she and fervent after love's heroism. She left me four years later for someone else. By a fine irony, it was the same midwinter that my lie came to light and the Milletts all invited me for Christmas just so they could disown me. That summer I can't remember whether I was planning on five hundred or a thousand dollars – but it was awfully goddamned ambitious. Had my john all picked out, friend of my rich aunt, owned a Cadillac agency, and was loaded, and, I thought, lecherous. Betting on the fresh youth angle. I never did get around to revealing my great scheme to him, but I did have the details pretty well worked out. I guess I was chicken: I was afraid he'd tell my folks. The factory was so monotonous, the assembly line such a nightmare, I woke up jibbering and sweating: I'd worked all summer and was still so far away from the $800 needed. There had to be a lot of money at once for passage and to satisfy customs. Harebrained scheme that it was, I was smart enough to know my body was all I had to trade on . I met a girl the other day who had actually sold herself for a woman she loved. Was the kid a better lover than I was (wit and determination enough not to settle on a friend of the family as her patron) – or was her beloved only a better tyrant ?

*

It seems to me that prostitution is somehow paradigmatic, somehow the very core of the female's social condition. It not only declares her subjection right in the open, with the cash nexus between the sexes announced in currency, rather than through the subtlety of a marriage contract (which still recognizes the principles of sex in return for commodities and historically has insisted upon it), but the very act of prostitution is itself a declaration of our value, our reification. It is not sex the prostitute is really made to sell: it is degradation. And the buyer, the john, is not buying sexuality, but power, power over another human being, the dizzy ambition of being lord of another's will for a stated period of time – the euphoric ability to direct and command an activity presumably least subject to coercion and unquestionably most subject to shame and taboo. This is a very considerable impression of power to purchase for ten or fifteen dollars. When the bargain is struck, the prostitute will, like labour in any exploitative relationship, try to do the least she possibly can to earn it. But at the same time the bargain *is* struck, and the very fact that it *can be* demonstrates the relative position of male and female, his place as master, hers as slave, outlined in a manner gross enough, enlarged enough, to evoke an earlier, more open mastery. Prostitution is, in a sense, antique, a fossil in the social structure, pointing, as all fossils do, to an earlier age. But the correct metaphor must be social, not phenomenological; must remind us, as Lévi-Strauss emphasizes, that men have traded in women throughout most of human history and have regarded her as currency in every country of the world, in societies where a monetary system was never arrived at. Little wonder that the origins of prostitution lie in temples converted from fertility rites to the cult of patriarchy.

Somehow every indignity the female suffers ultimately comes to be symbolized in a sexuality that is held to be her responsibility, her shame. Even the self-denigration required of the prostitute is an emotion urged upon all women, but rarely with as much success: not as frankly, not as openly, not as efficiently. It can be summarized in one four-letter world. And the word is not *fuck*, it's *cunt*. Our self-contempt originates in this: in knowing we are cunt. That is what we are supposed to be about – our essence, our offence.

Both the rewards and the punishment of accepting this definition are extravagant. J told me that in her prime, when she was really operating a business, she made $800 a week. With a Ph.D. and after ten years' experience in teaching, I was permitted to make only $60 a week. Since J and I are both academics, this amused us enormously. And we saw in it other kinds of prostitution such as those the academic world requires, the sycophancy due to department chairmen, the psychic blow jobs we call faculty meetings. But I know what the years in sexual prostitution have cost J too, can see it in the damage in her eyes, at moments their blueness as dead as glass. It is no melodious or pietistic bullshit to see prostitution as a particular crime against her humanity. Her suffering comes back when I remember our long halting talks, both her admissions and her denials, the long pained hours, her sensitive face. How much it has all hurt her: the years of silence and repression, the secrecy so deep it forbade her even to remember for some years after. And at the time, how deeply the pain required that she utterly anaesthetize herself, passive even to the point of numbness. Now too bitter to love anyone. That's a lot to pay even for $800 a week; it's a still more terrible sum for which to hold men liable.

For the prostitute, probably the ultimate oppression is the social onus with which she is cursed for accepting the agreed-upon social definition of her femaleness, her sexual abjectification. A Marxist analysis here is quite inadequate, as it fails to take psychological factors such as shame into account. For there is a crucial element quite beyond the economic. Perhaps it might be described as a kind of psychological addiction, to self-denigration, an addiction I feel all women are socially conditioned to accept. In a sexual culture as unhealthy as our own, it is reiterated again through the manner of our sexual acts that the female is carnality, a thing – cunt. It is as though cunt were posed as the opposite of ego or selfhood, its very antithesis, the negative pole of selfhood or spirit. The sale of women in prostitution reinforces this attitude more powerfully than any other event.

*

There is much cant about female masochism. One hears from males in general and Freudians in particular that it is congenital. One can recognize this as a hoax, a rationalization, knowing that any atrocity performed upon women is likely to be justified this way, with claims that self-defeating behaviour observed in women is organic, constitutionally female, inseparable from the x chromosome, and so forth. I am as annoyed as anyone when I hear such twaddle, and the very term irritates me as a deliberate misunderstanding. Yet I know that I behave 'masochistically' myself; I know that I continually make myself suffer in ways that men wouldn't think of. And I do it because masochism is part of the female role. It's feminine and I have been trained into it, even unconsciously. But this being the case, masochism is an inaccurate term altogether. If such utterly self-destructive behaviour is urged upon us, it is because our society is bent upon destroying something in its females, destroying their ego, their self-respect, their hope, their optimism, their imagination, their self-confidence, their will. 'Masochism' in such a group is, in fact, only the behaviour of accommodation, forced upon any oppressed group that it may survive. Because if members of this group do not so co-operate in their own oppression by interiorizing their oppressor's hatred and contempt, their insubordination will become apparent, and they will be punished and perhaps die. This is really not very difficult to understand if one observes the behaviour of other socially subordinate groups.

Prostitutes are bitter towards men and will often say they hate them. Given their relationships with men, how could they love them? It is difficult to see the prostitute's subjection to the measured sadism of the pimp pass for love by any criterion of emotional sanity. And so it is fairly common for prostitutes to love other women; women neither buy nor brutalize them (though it is not unknown for a prostitute to keep another woman as a pimp is kept, mimicking the heterosexual roles prevalent throughout society). In women, prostitutes seek the human acknowledgement men deny them and the tenderness our every custom denies men even learn. I'm told that in the House of Detention the women feel a curious serenity, often confessing that they enjoy going back. However absurd, this is a fantasy to which I find myself sympathetic. Somehow this fits our habit of self-abuse, happy when we are all locked up safe in our misery together. The prison is a secret home, asylum away from the pimp, away from the cop, away from dependency (you get fed in the House, and whenever you get fed you don't have to hustle). And there one is with other women, the one group of persons we flee most till we are confined together – at last a circumstance intervenes that justifies our hidden desires for association. Intimacy in inmateship. Even the defeatism of so arranging your life that the only time you are with other women is in prison is congruent with the repugnance for each other imposed on us by our training and situation. Yet for all one observes of it, one can still be overwhelmed at what women will do to themselves. Habits as well-learned as ours can be practised anywhere – proficiently at home or away.

*

This has been the most difficult bit of writing I've ever done, the most costly in time and psychic energy. Only to bring the people together was exhausting. It took most of the month of June; days and days of phoning; Byzantine diplomacy. Almost every woman knows someone in the life or someone who knows someone. But for people to come and talk is very very difficult; to ask them is difficult too. This summer's conversations were a long, strange experience, at first only puzzlingly traumatic. Fumio and I quarrelled with a terrible acrimony every night I held them, as if some inordinate resentment had taken hold of me and some overwhelming and surly defensiveness had found him, neither of which we understood. When the tapes were made I regarded them as precious. Then I found I could not even bear to listen to the tapes for two weeks after their completion. The experience had to settle down; I was very shaken by it. I found that it changed me a lot. I can hear it in the tapes, a continuous process from the first tapes where I talked all the time to the latter ones where I learned to listen a little. And there's a change in my voice from the usual excited voice one has at meetings, reserved for moments when everyone's trying to shout each other down, to a quieter voice, much quieter.

During the weeks we met at my studio I went along, day after day, driving myself, working twelve or twenty hours on an hour or two of rest, often none at all. Later I understood why I did it, and why the experience was so strangely unsettling. I think it wasn't only a feeling that we'd embarked on a great and possibly even dangerous project, but one that affected me at a level far deeper than conscious understanding. I mention all this because I venture that it has some larger meaning than just my own response, the emotions of an individual woman. You see, I began by saying I had an interest in prostitution because of this or that intellectual, social, or political concern. But it emerged in time that it was more than that – that prostitution was what I've called one of my 'closets'. Everyone has such closets in their mind that they're afraid to look into because they're terrifying. The notion of standing on Broadway offering myself to strangers, the idea of being that brave or desperate terrified me – terrifies me more than anything else I can think of. And the women who have been there and can tell me they've been through it do more than command my respect or imaginative understanding. It's almost as though they came back from having perpetuated the worst fantasy the rest of us harbour: our own nightmare.

The summer changed even my vision of the street and neighbourhood where I've lived for ten years. I can never see Third Avenue with the same indifferent innocence. One very hot day my ridiculous, elderly convertible chose to break down at the corner of Third Avenue and Thirteenth Street. While the transmission cooled I had a full hour to observe pimps, whores, and johns: what I had learned earlier in the summer made it like watching a foreign film a second time, after the dubbing had been added and one is able to understand the language. The pimps lean against a car smoking and overseeing trade; one fat and ugly, one with a shaved head, elegantly vicious. A great black woman jiggles herself on the threshold of a crummy bar. She is huge, ungainly. But she has a magnificent head. Young black culture hero in political costume, jacket, and shades, strolls past, catches sight of her, and with a superior turn of the head calls out an insult to the effect that she is a ton of meat, a heap of cunt.

She is stung, hurt out of the somnolence of her mindless and comforting dance of sale, and yells back 'sonofabitch', 'motherfucker'. But her clichés have no striking power, and he continues to taunt her, ridiculing the object for sale, cheapening it, defiling it, declaring it altogether valueless. All she has. Her outrage and frustration, the overpowering indignity make her shake. It's blown her cool altogether; she looks ashamed to live. The shouting has wakened a white hippie girl from her permanent high of down and she even throws out a curse at the guy. I astonish myself by yelling out at him, from the car, 'fuck off'. So we are a trio of women against this piece of arrogance. But he is untouched altogether (women are so contemptible) and saunters on, so righteous, so better, that it protects him like a celluloid covering.

Two big black birds on a black car, the pimps have never moved their eyelids. The whore is beaten. Later her master awards her a popsicle. The orange child-food glittering against her black shape in its black dress, she jiggles on. It was the fat guy who gave her the ice, but it was with the shaved head that I saw her again in Philadelphia at the Panther Conference. She was only along for the ride. It was the pimp, however, whom it was astonishing to meet at a 'Constitutional Convention of Revolutionary Peoples', resplendent in black beret, black leather jacket, complete with Panther badges. They are for sale – anyone can buy them – but the pimp as revolutionary is a repellent image. Yet not all that surprising either during that nightmare Philadelphia weekend when Panther swagger reached a fever pitch of macho bully.

Back to that scorched day on Third Avenue. One of the white prostitutes in the stable, unbelievably blank on heroin, walks back and forth almost blind. She uses herself like soiled Kleenex, dabbing at the traffic of uncurious males: a suit with a briefcase, two carpenters who snicker, a Puerto Rican whose cock-rank dictates that he bargain and then grandly refuse. It is 2.30 p.m. in the afternoon; the whores have eternity before them.

*

Another moment on Third Avenue, as the cab passes the Pocket Theatre at Twelfth Street, I thought I saw my younger sister, Mallory. I have a painful, surely over-protective obsession with Mallory's eventual victory over circumstances. This week she has another impossible job, taking tickets at the theatre. I look again. A quick cut: Mallory is transformed into a fourteen-year-old Puerto Rican whore standing by the entrance. Today might be Mallory's day off, but not this kid's. How easily has the child's slavery come about, how acceptable people find it – her fellowmen. It's 11.30 a.m. in the morning. Will a john have her for lunch? My older-sister's fury feeds on his gizzard.

Then one fine summer evening when things were going splendidly, the tin can even a joy to drive, and some happy meeting with a friend lighting my euphoria, I pulled up at the corner of Third and Thirteenth. That first corner. Both women were there. I'm recognized by two prostitutes' long stare. Suddenly I feel extremely derelict in duty; just what duty I have no idea. But it seems criminal to be in such a mellow mood, so rich feeling, even though I'm broke, the movie having consumed every cent I can get my hands on. Even the uncertain mobility of this old car seems a luxury, wildly extravagant. What's expected of me anyway – saintly fanaticism? What new absurdity am I getting myself into, I wonder, recognizing the traps of white liberal and middle-class guilt spread out before me. I've enough lower-mid in me to encumber my life with an infatuation for a real greaser's car. And I am not forced to recover from a Seven Sister's education through courses in home explosives like Bryn Mawr's poor dead child.

I've seen class guilt send movement women into frenzies of divisiveness all year, poisoning the hopes of unity with a self-righteous missionary trip, which maunders on about the Third World and proletarian woman, using it as an opportunity for endless recriminations among former friends, all of them middle-class. The animosity we practise upon each other is ultimately little better than a form of self-multilation. It is a habit now among that social group who might be described as bourgeoisie in origin transformed into the masses upon arrival into the New Left. A righteous political asperity or a dedication to violent means and manners is here a guarantee of sincerity, even atonement, for the comfort of one's upbringing. This sort of meddling folly would delight in converting the prostitute into flag and symbol, a movement idol. Where scores are kept, with the highest Oppression Rating awarded the most acrimonious effusion, the whore's penultimate suffering could be quickly and facilely converted into a super-rating.

But the two prostitutes are still staring at me. And whatever that stare means, it's recognition. They know me from last time, know I watched and saw their experience, know I know whatever little I know. Ignorance may be a lousy excuse, but at least it's something. When you lose it you gain responsibility. And if you have knowledge of something as wrong as their wrongs and do nothing, you take on some culpability, even complicity.

The traffic light changes colour and the car turns home. But I have felt that stare and registered it. M says there is danger in continuing the project, swears the pimp is smart enough to figure out the economic threat women's liberation could offer him if we had any success in reaching prostitutes. She warns that like any capitalist he'll be uptight if hit in the pocket. And since like any pimp he specializes in beating up women, some of us might be attacked if we were successful. I'm a fairly frank physical coward, and the prospect of being worked over sometime by a couple of pimps does terrify me. It is for that reason (among others, but the others are only variant dreams of an end to black male chauvinism) I look forward to the possibility of Panther support, counting on one muscle man against the other, hoping they cancel each other out, so that women, black and white, may be able to come together, free of the bully pimp. And of course the Panthers could do it if they chose – could pass the word that pimping was out, over, unacceptable, uncool. If they really felt that way.

Beyond acting as a catalyst I know I can do little myself. There are a number of women who have worked with me on this project and who now care about it quite a lot; the women who compose the quartet, of course, but others too who came to our raps and contributed a knowledge of persons, or prisons, or law. I feel very strongly that the discussions must be continued and enlarged. It will be the prostitutes themselves, the persons involved and informed, who are best qualified to direct the decisions and strategy of such a campaign and its targets: the vice squad, city hall, the legislature. At present prostitutes are subject to arrest at any moment, stigmatized in any area of employment by a record and fingerprints, and offered no protection against the assaults of pimps or police. Again, it would be the prostitutes themselves who are in the best position to direct young movement lawyers, law students, and legal assistants towards those incidents in the prostitute's life that would make the most promising test-case material in a long-range legal struggle, not only to change the present laws so oppressive to prostitutes, but to extend every form of civil rights to a group so long and so generally denied them.

*

Prostitution has flourished always and made fortunes, counting on and aided by the state. Considering the weight of this tradition, one gets a notion of how heavy a job actual social revolution is: bigotry, habit, moneyed interest, physical force, even indifference are so solid. How unshakably based in these things our man's world really is. To look ahead nearly takes one's breath away – the difficulty of the thing. Just the mess our sick culture has made of sexuality. Yet one can think of a love that's free based on respect, affection, understanding, tenderness. How great to live that way. And to love many people and love them well. To have the joy of that, of what love is without possessiveness, exclusiveness, jealousy, property, economic dependence, ego conflict. How full of flowers, music, highs, conversation, fantastic love making . . . all of it could be. And I think it's worth it. But never let it prevent you from the knowledge and expectation of how hard it's going to be, how scary – until we can live that way. And it's not only the hedonist but the pragmatist that urges we practise for living the revolution, since surely there won't be one unless we've made some progress at living the new way. And it must be new: revolution's got to be a better way to live, lovingly even. Not hate: we have such a sickening amount of that already.

But all of it will hardly be easy. I had a glimpse of that this spring. It was after the abortion rally and some of us went down to the Women's House of Detention. The Panther women are being held there, and the custom had grown up over the winter of ending most demonstrations in the city there. It was strangely exciting – even the walk from Union Square – you knew so well where you were going that you picked up a feeling for it as you went along. It was a feeling for what we'd see there. Not just the cops all lined up making trouble, but the place itself. We were headed for the big place our lives are supposed to be spent not heading for, going to it by a new route.

I can remember asking some of my friends among the women at the rally if they were going down. Some said yes, some said not this time, next time, or I'll be there soon. Kidding about it. But aware it may not be a joke long. Robin and Ti-Grace and some others have already been there, busted at a peaceful sit-in against Grove Press. In a sense one somehow expects the House of D. eventually; a premonition, a sense of foreknowing, we'll get together there someday. Most days I remember this is paranoia and that a claustrophobe like myself is bound to be fascinated and frightened of places like this. But that late afternoon in March after the rally and the march and the crowds and the chanting it all made a curious logic.

So we arrived. We're on the far side of the street so we can see up at the walls. The prostitutes, the shoplifters, and the addicts in the House of Detention are on the other. And the cops between us. Two groups of women with men and walls intervening. We're yelling, of course. But so are they across the street. The most astonishing thing: they're yelling political stuff. It blew my mind. 'Free our sisters,' we're chanting. And they're echoing it back. Then they're chanting it and we're echoing it back. But they're talking to us: we're communicating at last. And in between us, between the two groups, the men, the police.

Look up and the women are all at the windows. I once worked in a lock-up, had a job in a mental hospital the summer I was eighteen. I've carried my bunch of keys, and

I know that when everybody's at the windows like this – everything's out of control. They are keeping them inside the building, but it seems sure that they're beyond the pale in there – way out of hand. They're all there at the windows where we can hear them and see them. Not just a random voice heard by a shopper on Sixth Avenue carrying groceries along, the prisoner yelling something for the crowd to laugh at. Every single woman in the place seems to be at the windows, shouting.

I looked up at this building. It's so big and so strong and so made out of stone. I begin to see how hard revolution is. Because we can shout free our sisters till we crumble and there's still that stone wall between us, the iron security entrance, and all those cops. They won't crumble. You get a notion of what you're up against.

Seeing it all, a strange perception came over me. That prostitutes are our political prisoners – in jail for cunt. Jailed for it, for cunt, the offence we all commit in just being female. That's sexual politics, the stone core of it.

M

Now I'm off the street. And if a cop comes up to me and sticks his hand in my shirt, feeling me up to look for something, you can believe it baby I'm gonna call a lawyer or the ACLU or something. But in those days it was pretty different. I was holding then and likely to carry heroin in my bra. And when you got that shit on you, you don't argue. If they don't get you for drugs, they'll get you for whoring. And you gotta be scared all the time. Now I can tell him to get his fucking hand off me. I got myself together now.

You can say whoring is business. Or a means to an end. But it's not that cut and dried. It's important for you to know that most women who turn tricks have to be loaded on something. You don't have any woman out there selling this commodity and doing this trading who's not loaded on something. They're not that hip to business. And they're not that void. Like you gotta have something. If you're not high on dope it's something else. Every time I went to turn a trick I had to fix before and after. There's a price a woman pays.

One of the problems we deal with in drug rehabilitation is to get women to have a little pride, get up off the floor. We have to cope with the feeling of having turned a trick. This is one thing that stays with women and makes them feel very bad about themselves. The fact that at one time in their lives they were in a position where they were out selling their bodies. They really have one hell of a time forgetting about that.

Prostitution goes with addiction. Because it's a means of supporting a habit. Something that'll sell when nothing else will. I don't think you ever get too sick or too ragged or too ugly or too beat up to turn a trick. There's always someone out there buying. But you can get too beat up or raggedy to go to a store and try to boost something. They chase you out. And whoring is also a fast way to make enough money for a bag.

When I was using it, about eight or nine years ago, heroin was five dollars. Now it's gone up. And there's no limit on the bags you need. You need as many bags as you can get, depending only on the amount of money you can find. I used about $100 a day. If you've got $15 a day, you use that; if you've got $50, you use that; if you've got $100, you use $100. You use whatever you make. It's a trap.

There's usually something left for a place to sleep and some food, unless you're living with a man. Around this neighbourhood if you can get enough together for a bag, you can just sleep on a roof someplace. But most junkies live in rooms. You can scrape enough up for a room most days. And you live on hero sandwiches, Yoo-Hoos, candy bars, that kind of thing – cupcakes, kid food. The food of regression; addiction itself is a form of regression. The drug becomes the nourishment you receive through your veins.

You can say prostitution feeds a drug habit. Which comes first? Perhaps it's a kind of circle. You need the shit to kill the pain of prostitution; you need the prostitution to kill the pain of needing the drug. Around and around. But generally addiction comes first in most cases. Most people come to find themselves associated with drugs, the underworld, and so they naturally find themselves associated with prostitution, prostitutes, and pimps. I was into drugs first. When you start on drugs you start hanging out in certain places and with a certain kind of people.

I lived the first twenty years of my life around nuns and a convent. And the first heroin I ever saw in my life I used. I don't think I was rebelling. It was the point in my life when my family broke into pieces – like my father and about the fifth wife he'd had during the twenty years I'd lived with him finally separated. We had a house and a car and that whole bit, and it all went down the drain.

My father pretty much raised me. And I think I was kinda thrown, disappointed and rollin'. My father was a drinker and not too well put together. I think my step-mother just couldn't take him anymore. So they separated. And for the first time in my life I felt I was some sort of outcast. She didn't take me with her. Most of my father's women spent all their time resenting my relationship with him. Like I say, I felt myself thrown out in the street, depressed and upset about the whole thing, the separation. I had to learn to take care of myself. That's what was going down with me. Nobody had ever taught me how to make it in the street. I grew up in the convent instead. Did you ever hear that song of Bobby Dylan's – 'Like a Rolling Stone?' It was like that.

> How does it feel to be on your own
> No direction known
> Like a rolling stone
> Nobody ever taught you how to make it on the street
> Now you'll have to get used to it.

Well, nobody ever taught me how to make it in the street. I just did it on my own. And I made my way. I really don't believe in the bullshit they teach you in the Catholic Church – that if you do good you get good, love your neighbour, and you're your brother's keeper and all that bullshit. You're a mark for everybody. They laugh at you, and they lay you. I was a marked woman. I mean like when I started using drugs. I didn't know the price of a bag. I didn't even know how to hit myself with the needle.

And I was stealing at that point. Compared to boosting, I was a lousy whore. I was really a lousy whore. That wasn't my shtick at all. I was a good thief though. I used to make $200 a day, then give it all to some guy. I used to take orders, like Petricelli suits – that's an Italian name-brand suit. Got them from men's clothing stores. But you can't boost with no shopping bag. That's not cool. You have to wear something loose. You wear something very very loose, not some tight-fitting dress. Like you have to put it between your legs and under your arms. First thing, you have to roll it to make it very small and compact so you can stash it on the body. I used to take orders from people. They used to tell me what they wanted and I'd go get it.

Boosting didn't frighten me too much. I guess in the beginning I was a little worried. A girl friend and I used to go boosting for fun, just daring. I was nervous too. Stuff like mink stoles, stuff like that. I got busted. I got busted a couple of times but it don't freeze you up. Because you've *got* to make money. So you change territories.

I could dress well enough so I could pass in those places. That's very important. Also you've got to have a car. Very important to have a car when you're boosting. You dress nice, you have a car. Very 'bouge' looking, which is an accomplishment because usually when you walk into a store, if they're looking, you're *black*, no matter how well dressed you are. Very often I'd team up with some white girl and the heat was off. Then you could clean up.

They don't say, 'Excuse me, lady, are you shoplifting?' They usually say, 'Can I help you please?' And are very insistent about it. It's frightening, but I think the most important thing is that you can't panic. You have to remember never to panic because the moment you panic, you're *dead*. You have to be very cool, you have to defend yourself. Of course you deny everything, that you're not copping nothing. As long as they don't catch you with the goods on you. Even if they catch you with the goods on you in the store, you can still cop out. But what they usually do is let you get outside, and if they get you outside you're dead. You've had it at that point. Still, you can pretend like you don't know what's happening. 'Who, me?' And then you have a lawyer who you keep and pay, that you can call and you get away with a fine.

Having a lawyer, being smart, this makes it easier. You get out of jail faster and you can make more money. But I didn't always do that good. Like the last year when I was into addiction, I was grimy, came out of the bottom of the barrel. You can't keep it up. Because the heroin becomes too demanding, and you can't have time for all that bullshit, for making the rounds, being cool, and so on. You don't have time for all that. You have to work something out. But there's a trap you fall into once you get started and you're doing really good. I used to hang around uptown a lot, like at Minton's. It's a bar at 118th Street at St Nicholas and Seventh Avenue. That's where Charlie Parker, Miles Davis, and a lot of those guys hung out. It's a place where all the real hustlers are, guys that blow $1,000, you know – pimps and everything. I've been in and out of there a lot and I was young. They used to like me and spent a lot of money on me. The pimps. Pimps spend on some women. Sure they do. They used to give me a lot of coke – a lot of cocaine. But once you start on that heroin, they don't have anything to do with you after that. But the whole point was I really thought I was into something, boosting, and it was going to go on for ever that way. I was always going to be like really into something cool and high rollin' and everything. But that's not true. Not with that heroin. Heroin's not like amphetamines. I think speed affects your brain and stuff like that. Heroin doesn't have that kind of effect on you. Heroin's just the opposite, it's like a depressant – I mean it's real down. That's why when people take an overdose their heart stops beating and it slows down your heart like to nothing – poop, poop, poop. Like nothing's happening.

It's a groove. If you were rich and could afford it and didn't have to work in the street and do things . . . You see, heroin doesn't get you arrested; it's what you have to *do* to get the heroin that gets you arrested. Heroin's not bad for your body. There's no physical defect as a result of using heroin. What happens to people's bodies is that if they're reefing heroin they don't go to the dentist. They don't go to the doctor. If you're rich and went to the doctor and you kept yourself up and you could afford heroin, it'd be a real groove. You could be totally out of it all the time. Not feeling, not knowing.

People do feel high on heroin. And you can even get a lot done. You know, musicians play. Charlie Parker played better. You can write on it. I know some actors who're acting on it, but they won't be for very long. 'Course if you're rich and have somebody there to take care of you – be O.K. If the stuff cost just as much as cigarettes and was legal, be no problem.

There was a panic five years ago when there was no drugs in the street. I never knew the details, heard it through the grapevine. There was a whole thing going between Genovese and Robert Kennedy. Bobby was trying to get him. Genovese said something like 'I'll show you what'll happen if I take all the stuff out of the street. Try to put a stop to it.' During a panic you really find out who's on dope. Because everyone comes out looking for a bag – chauffeur-driven Cadillacs, Mercedes Benzes, people you never thought was using heroin before, you find out: they come out like dogs. So it's a simple matter of a bag and who can afford it. If you can afford it you got it made, and you're not going to have to hustle or go uptown trying to get it. If you don't have money, somebody's gonna come and get you. Put you in jail. And then you don't have money for someone to get you out. And then you become a statistic.

You can say – well, if they didn't make a racket out of it. Well, can I tell you something? There's a lot of money involved in heroin, so they'll never make it legal and it'll never be abolished. And when there's that much money involved, forget it.

*

I'll bet legalizing prostitution would take a lot of wind out of its sails too. But in Nevada prostitution *is* legal and they have more murders and . . . No, I don't think they should legalize prostitution. Anyway, I don't dig those state whore-houses. In Reno they have legal whorehouses, and they have them in Hamburg too. Everyone walks around with a licence. If you ever tried to get another job, forget it. They've got you on the police books, and the state is making a lot of money on prostitution. Cool. Got it? And then the second thing is, like you're in there. You're really in a box, because they've got you licensed and ticketed and you can't do anything else. In Hamburg you can't appear on the streets in the rest of the city, in the nice part, after 8 p.m. so you're on a reservation, in a cell. In the Near East the brothels are literally cages, and whores have to turn twenty to thirty tricks a day.

My first experience with prostitution was in a whore-house, and you're in a cage no matter which way you look at it. That was a real dragged-out horror; I'll never forget that as long as I live. I was taken there by some old woman who was a prostitute, who was teaching me to be a prostitute. She'd been a prostitute since she was about thirteen years old; her name was Djuna Mae. So she was going to teach me to be a prostitute. She went through the whole thing of taking me to her room, showing me how to give head and all that. So she finally took me to this whorehouse in Trenton, New Jersey. This place was too much to believe. The police, the detectives used to come every day for their payoff. They used to talk to the madam of the house; they'd pick up their money and leave. Only white men came into this place. Right in the middle of Trenton.

The girls were all black, with a few exceptions. Not entirely all black. There were a few exceptions. Variety. Very important – variety in a whorehouse. And you'd just sit there. A guy would come in; he'd look everybody over and he'd pick you and you'd go off to the room. You could never see your money. The madam would demand the money, and when you got ready to leave she would give you your half. I decided after three days it wasn't for me. I didn't like it, and I wanted to leave. And she didn't have my money. She'd gambled it away. Later found out that if I had a pimp she would have given me my money. He would have threatened her. I didn't have a man who was a pimp who could kick her ass, or whatever they do.

So I didn't get my money, but I really wasn't uptight for money because I still had money in the bank, you know what I mean. Didn't really need to go to this whorehouse 'cause I had money in the bank, but I was doing something *different*. It was a whole different *scene* for me. I wasn't on the street. I was getting experience. I romanticized this sort of shit.

I was real impressed with Djuna Mae and this homosexual Bernard. I used to stop by their house every morning. They lived between my house and my church. After a while I'd start for Djuna Mae's, and they'd give me grass and then they'd talk about the money they made and doing their thing. They were very cool people and I was very impressed. Djuna Mae made it sound so groovy to go to this whorehouse. I could make money and that was where it was at. And besides, I was trying very hard to impress her. To show her that I had guts. I dug her. I liked Djuna Mae. I gave her the first heroin she ever had in her life. She was an older woman. She'd never used heroin in her life. She's been in the street for years. She stuck with it. I never thought of it as revenge. I was turning her on like she was turning me on.

A lot of people go into the street on a dare, or for kicks, or to prove something. I mean, like when I think about how goddamned naive I was. I went from the convent to the streets. But they aren't that far apart, because evil had a glamour for me. And I thought Djuna Mae was cool. But you can bet that was some ugly whorehouse. Oh god, it was horror. I wound up burning that goddamned whorehouse down. And going to jail. I actually burned it down. It was a matter of principle. I wanted my money. Every time I went back and asked for my money, she was never there. And I thought: 'The bitch is in there and she's coming out!'

I watched the fire. It was a real groove. The flames were leapin' out all over. I didn't want to kill her; I just wanted to see her come out. They knew I did it. Arthur knew it. I had a lawyer. The DA was a Catholic. It was a 'house of sin'. I was facing five to twenty years. But I got out of it pretty cool.

This place looked very legitimate from the outside. A friend of mine says half of the air-conditioned apartments in New York are whorehouses. I could have made a lot of money. Eight hundred dollars, or half of that – if she'd paid up.

*

If you're gonna whore you need protection: a man's protection from other men. All men are in the protection business. We don't need protection from women: if men didn't beat us up we wouldn't need half the husbands we got. You know, most whores don't even get laid by their pimps. Most of them in a stable never get laid at all. There's usually one who does. He usually has a favourite; if he doesn't have a favourite in the stable he usually has a favourite across town some place. There's always a woman some place he spends money on. But there has to be a lesbian or someone in a stable to take care of you sexually.

Pimps got to save themselves for driving their Cadillacs. They cheat on us. They're women-haters. They have a very low opinion of the women in the stable. Who ever respected his slaves? And I think probably a lot of them have a very difficult time getting it up anyway. Because that's a very important thing with a pimp – you do *not* fuck. You do not fuck. You just make money. You don't fuck women: you make money off of them. Like women are like employees. What if the pimp really had to satisfy the whole stable?

Say she comes in and she needs a little loving – like to be loved – that takes a couple of hours. Say he had to do that five times a night. The bastard would be dead in the morning. And anyway, he's got to drive his Cadillac. Heavy work. He's got to brag to the other pimps and that takes some energy. Hang around in bars. Pimps look and act like most other men. They're the same as any men are with each other. When men get together men are like men. They flex their muscles, talk about their conquests, and their bitches. The language might vary from place to place or the words might be a little different, but they do the same thing when they get together at Small's as they do at the Playboy Club.

And pimps make and spend a lot of money. They spend a helluva lot of money. I mean, to spend $1,000, $2,000 a day is nothing for a pimp. They party. A pimp's whole life is a party. They do most of their partying with other pimps. The *real* people. Not the broads who make the money, mere employees. Pimps go play golf together. They have fun with one another. A lot of them are some of the most handsome, intelligent guys. They have to be. You can't be an idiot and be a pimp. An idiot can't be a pimp and pull it off successfully. He's going to get it. And it's true, any guy who's a good pimp would be a good banker. They're in business. And the best pimps come from the South. It's very interesting; they make the best hustlers too. Guys from the South, they make the best con men. I think it's because nobody suspects them; everyone thinks they're stupid. It's a fence game. They even fool black people with that shit, the country boy act. But that whole pimp–whore thing is something else. I didn't ever have a pimp. No, I can't say that. Yes I did. I rationalize mine away because he was my man. Because there was nobody else but me that I know of – no stable. I selected him without making him my pimp. But I guess I made him into my child instead.

It's a whole game. When a pimp is trying to pull a girl into the stable, I think he does a bit of romancing and spending and everything like that. And once he gets her, he keeps on promising. There's a book based on interviews with a pimp called Iceberg Slim, very accurate account of the whole scene. Prostitutes admire pimps. They'll kill for them. Then they'll turn around and kill the pimp too. They do kill pimps sometimes. There's always a great amount of fear when you have slaves about. Fear of what will happen to you.

Pimps do rotten things. I guess they have to. That life is kind of bitter. And if you're in that life, how else are you gonna be a pimp? And live up to it? You've got to prove everything all over every day, right? You've got all the guys watching you. What do they do? What kinds of really raunchy things do they do? What are they capable of, these cats? I saw a girl walk into a bar and hand the pimp a $100 bill. He took it and burned it in her face and turned around and knocked her down on the floor and kicked her and said, 'I told you, bitch, $200. I want $200, not $100.' Now she's gotta go out again and make not another hundred, but two hundred. I know of some pimps who killed a whore with an overdose of heroin and then fucked her dead body. They're sick. Half the time they're not in their right minds – out on coke or something. It's a special world they live in.

Getting into turning tricks after the way I grew up, the convent and all – I was always aware of a certain amount of guilt. Always guilty. All that guilt. But once I started I was kind of like *in* it. After the first time it was all over. 'Cause then I had lost face, so what the hell. Everybody knew. And when I burned down that whorehouse I made the Trenton papers. I was scared and guilty, but I got a kick out of it too. Both emotions at once. Got a real bang out of it. Got arrested: never been arrested before. Like a movie. Me and my girl friend. Set the fire and called the fire department. Then this big deal of getting out of town in the back of a car, and policemen. I was eighteen. I have no idea where she is now, my girl friend.

She was from Perth Amboy. I go to Asbury Park and I still see people I knew when I was in the streets. Occasionally here in New York I meet somebody I knew when I was in the streets. I still see some gay guy I used to hustle with when I was in Connecticut. I haven't seen him in a while. I wonder what happened to him. He was a friend of mine. There were a few people who were real friends. But there isn't much room for friendship in that world. Though there are some people who are all right no matter what. Not much space for love either.

People can't trust each other much in that world. You need the drug so badly you'll do anything. And there are so many games and roles; mommy and daddy and kid games. You need each other only 'cause there's nobody and nothing else.

It's going to be hard to change this system. Black men are into a special macho thing now that goes well with the system of exploitation we call pimps and whores. It may not be 'legitimate' for white women rather than black women to approach the black liberation guys with this. But that's where their heads are at now. They'd listen to white women faster. Black men might do a lot about prostitution if they thought they could stop white men from coming uptown and turning a trick. They could stop putting black women out on corners. The women they are calling whores, the women they hate, the women who they say got no class, and are all the things they don't want, those are the women they keep sticking out on the corner. Most of those guys uptown that keep sticking black women out on corners get into their El Dorado and go downtown, and spend most of her money on some eighteen- or nineteen-year-old little white girl. She's a lady 'cause she went to a fancy school and her folks are white bread. That's racism. Doing Whitey's thing. Charlie's nigger. Fucking Charlie's daughter. And you know he ain't doing that white girl no good either. Getting back at Charlie through women. Putting both women down. Since childhood that's what he's seen Charlie do. Can't do nothing else, 'cause Charlie's his sole model. He *has* no other. The white man is the *only* man. And that's why he tries to get a Cadillac and a white woman. Then he'll have everything Charlie got.

You give a black woman to a black man and she'll remind him of his mother who he wanted desperately to get away from. She's spent a great part of her time doing what he calls 'suppressing' him, that is, keeping him from being a white man. It's all about power and all about Charlie. Charlie runs everything, runs the white women too. He owns it all.

L

Just to remember that year in the courts brings back my depression, the futility I knew every day, the impotence . . . Last year I was with the Vera Institute of Justice, trying to provide civil rights counsel at arraignments. I had felt that if I were to be working with accused persons, I wanted to be working with women. From the time I started, even when I was up in the Bronx, the women I saw in the court were just so much more sad, really wasted people than the men. Somehow the kinds of crime men were involved in did not seem to devastate them as much. Crime has in it a curiously gratifying element of macho for a man: a hustler, con, hood. To a woman crime is a terrifying sort of breakthrough, degrading to a kind of ingrained self-image of femininity.

Logically, I started to see prostitution as the form of criminal activity not only most prevalent among women in the numbers arraigned, but also as representing the most awful kind of life a woman might have. Or so it seemed at the time. I would never say it is the most honest life for a woman because that implies a value judgement on my part about what is honest. But it is surely the most obvious way in which women sell themselves: using themselves as commodity, being used as commodity. Really being just that – and that being the most appropriate possible metaphor for our whole condition. I think of crime itself as a notion, a concept representing those things a society holds most dear and yet is most afraid of. The fact that sex is directly linked to money only through prostitution represents the devious way in which society deals with its truths.

I started thinking what it would be like to be a prostitute, what it would be like to be in prison for it, what it would be like to live as a prostitute. I started reading things – stuff written mostly by men. Except for Sara Harris who argued that women were able to separate sex and love, that prostitution was simply a business, and claimed that there was no higher incidence of homosexuality among prostitutes, that it was just another way that a woman could live. And deep, in some very basic woman's part of me, I said, 'No, that's not true. It's as degrading for them as it is for me to sleep with someone I don't care about and wake up in the morning next to him.' Then I began to realize that the difference lay in my expectation about what might happen when I woke in the morning; my expectations were very different from those of a woman who was selling herself, a woman who was hustling. The fact that she was turning a trick on him, rather than being turned and exploited by her own emotions, came home to me. Because in her case nothing would ever meet those expectations of intimacy the act presupposed – and this made it very different: she could not be disappointed, and I could. So when I first started to write about prostitution, the distance that I felt between her condition and my own was enormous.

Months in the courts gave me an idea for a project of my own, a rehabilitation centre for women convicted of crime and run by such people themselves, as the drug rehabilitation centres are. I finally succeeded in convincing the Vera Institute to let me draw up such a plan and work out its details. But it too became a disappointment – restricted by its very nature: establishment funding and the process of remanding women from the court which would make the women prisoners of the programme. What I have now is a nearly settled conviction of impossibility, a knowledge it is impossible to relate to women this way. Finally perhaps impossible to relate at all. I see these women in the court every day, and I feel they are my sisters. But how deep the barriers are, how deep their defences. And so ingrained in our sense of ourselves as women is the idea of sexual objectification, that I see these women and I don't even begin to know how to speak with them. And I feel not only that my presuppositions, but even my analysis and judgements on prostitution, come out of something I'm prevented from realizing in any way.

The actual situation in the city is that prostitution is accepted by everyone – police, judges, clerks, and lawyers. Arrest and prosecution are purely gestures that have to be made to keep up the façade of public morality. The method of dealing with it is simply a form of harassment, not a form of prevention, abolition, or punishment. There is no conviction at any level that prostitution is a crime on anyone's part, only a total and satisfied acceptance of the double standard, excusing the male, accusing the female. There is also a curious fascination with the prostitutes, 'the girls', a geniality towards them, friendliness even, in the sense of familiarity.

What was most frightening to me in court was not only my own sense of distance, of separation from the women arraigned, but the very familiarity, as I said, between the clerks, the judges, the women themselves, everyone in the court. Everyone accepts the fact that each woman who comes in will be in again and again, will go through the same routine, maybe stay in the pens overnight, but she knows all the cops and they know her, they accept her and they fuck her and she pays them and gets off: that's how the relationship is defined, clear and simple. And I play no part in the scheme at all. It's obvious to all that prostitution should be made legal, obvious to the women themselves that prostitutes suffer for the supposed crimes of other people, yet the guilt and shame are part of their lives as well, their isolation too: all this is made clear in talking to them. The distance I feel from the women when I'm in court, the familiarity with which they relate to the men – the clerks, the judges, the cops – is so heartbreaking to me that I don't know how to bear it.

I feel utterly paralyzed as I sit in the arraignment part computing the numbers of women who are getting fucked over for one thing or another, and a prostitute walks in, heavily made up, heavily wigged, wearing supposedly seductive clothes, open, friendly and warm, flirting with all the rest of the people – all the men. There's my sister and I'm so far removed from her.

When it is understood that I am one of the women who wishes to work with prostitutes, the attitude I am received with becomes one of incredulous ridicule on the part of every member of the court, ranging all the way from male clerks to male Legal Aid people. Even women Legal Aid people and the other women around, the women who are legal secretaries. Everyone assures me I'll fail; everyone is eager to set me straight: 'You'll never be able to relate to them. How could they want to give it up when they make so much money? How could you ever talk to them?' And for months my innate sense of idealism and sisterhood said 'No, that's not true. There's a solidarity among us that can break through that.' Yet sitting in the court every day, or interviewing women in the pens and feeling paralyzed while interviewing, in dread even about what this may tell you of how hopeless I feel it is, knowing that the shell these women have developed about their lives as women, about their relationships to men, about their relationships to the pimps (who are there with them, bailing them out) goes so much deeper than any sense of potential solidarity I feel or that the woman's movement could give now.

Finally I've come to feel that the whole legal system backs men up, confirms their power. In court I've been watching what happens to women who are picked up for prostitution. There are some judges who will just dismiss it. The district attorney will charge the woman with loitering for the purposes of prostitution, and the judge will respond with,

'Forget it, this is pointless.' Other judges will send prostitutes up for fifteen to ninety days. It is a system which says that women who are making it with men for money, selling their body when it is the best, the only, commodity they have, are commiting a victimless crime, but, nonetheless, we're going to get them for it. And for me, there's no clearer indication than prostitution that all women are a potential species of social or political prisoner. Prostitution is really the only crime in the penal law where two people are doing a thing mutually agreed upon and yet only one, the female partner, is subject to arrest. And they never even take down the man's name. It's not his crime, but the woman's.*

Anyone who believes to some extent in the basic tenets of women's liberation has probably also believed that in some way prostitutes are the most exploited of women. And there has been much rhetoric on how prostitutes are the most oppressed among us, how in a sense they are models for the movement because most exploited, because engaged in work that is the most direct and honest expression of our general condition, prostitution putting the economic relationship between the sexes 'right out front' and so forth. All of this, in an abstract way, does make sense to me. But I know too that when I go down every day to those pens below the court where the women are kept, all this no longer makes sense to me at all. Because all I see are the wrecks of what society has done to these particular individuals. I could rap to them about women's lib stuff for hours. And they are so out of touch with themselves, they cannot hear. Even if you assume that there's a sense of rage which develops, you can scarcely continue with that assumption when you see their terrible passivity, their remoteness from any consciousness of their condition.

*

* The recent New York statute, which declares the male client (the 'john') guilty too, in an act of female prostitution, is simply not enforced and may therefore be disregarded in such discussions.

Since I've been in court, I've seen cases of women who have been arrested for years and years for nothing but prostitution – thirty-five, forty arrests in a year, maybe. Just back and forth, coming in and out. There's one lawyer I've seen do all the expensive prostitution grabs, an old, grey-haired, greasy, pin-stripe-suited guy, making all his money off women. But he's always the one they want. I don't know whether his offices are in the court and he just sits there and waits, or whether he goes into the pens and picks up cases, or whether he's known to all, or what the situation is, but he deals with all the prostitution cases where a lawyer is hired, all the cases that Legal Aid doesn't get, all the cases where a woman wants to get out quickly.

Few women actually go on trial for prostitution. Charged only with loitering, most simply plead guilty at arraignment and pay their fine, ranging from $15 to $100. Almost none of the women I've seen, maybe two, have had to go to the House of Detention because they were unable to pay their fine right on the spot. And a good three quarters of the time cases are simply dismissed.

The charge of prostitution itself, which was once merely a violation, is now a misdemeanour in New York, a heavier charge with a longer maximum sentence. The change was made at the recommendation of the Mayor's Committee on Prostitution. It is interesting that the only woman who served on this committee was a person connected in some capacity with the House of Detention. The committee's justification in lengthening the maximum penalty for prostitution was that there would be a longer period for rehabilitation in prison, the old sentence of fifteen days being far too short a time to effect change. Originally, in fact until two or three years ago, there was a separate court called Women's Court. But prostitutes are now arraigned in the regular arraignment part of the Criminal Court, like all other criminals.

In actual practice, raising the charge of prostitution to a misdemeanour has, paradoxically, actually softened it.

What happens is this: the district attorney, who in the Complaint Room has the discretion (given the evidence that the policeman will submit) to charge a woman with a particular crime, is astute enough to know that if his office overcharges – if for instance, his office charges a woman with prostitution, when the only evidence it has is for loitering – the judge will raise hell and throw it out of court. So the practice has simply been to lay a charge of loitering rather than one of prostitution. And in nearly every loitering case I've watched, the district attorney dismisses charges. What this means is that a woman may be picked up and literally come into court and walk right out. Generally, however, she is picked up at night and locked up in the pens overnight until arraigned. Even when she escapes the fine through dismissal of charges, she has been harassed. When she is fined in addition, she has contributed to the support of the system that oppresses her. It also means that there is no systematic attempt to enforce the new prostitution law with its intention of longer periods of rehabilitation. Instead, the effect is only a continuous intimidation and inconvenience placed upon prostitutes – and a continuous fleecing.

Almost none of the women I've seen actually committed to the House of Detention have been charged with prostitution, but with other crimes. They may and do hustle, but that isn't what they're being picked up for. And every woman I've seen who comes in to pay bail comes in with a man, so one may be sure there is still a very active pimp trade. What is being done lately, however, is a good deal more sinister than jailing whores. Prostitutes are being imprisoned through a kind of preventive detention on other grounds than prostitution itself: namely petty theft and drugs, the two areas where prostitutes are most likely to have previous records or might 'reasonably' be expected to be future offenders – the two crimes prostitutes most often resort to to supplement or to palliate their prostitution. So while prostitution itself is hardly prosecuted, prostitutes themselves are imprisoned and subject to the specious, and unjustifiable – often even capricious – methods of preventative detention.

In the court itself the women concentrate their attentions upon the men who will judge or release them, the battery of male officials at whose mercy they are – the Man who will decide their fate. It is only in the pens, the cages in the basement of the building, that the women are together as women, and the pens reveal the way women relate to each other. In the pens there is a strange hilarity; the women rap and talk to each other. The comfortableness between the women there is a stark contrast to the way they ignore each other when upstairs in the court itself. They seem open to each other, apparently familiar with each other too. It's a kind of laughing, giggling, crazy high scene, like when they are outside, or just paying their fine, finished and on their way out. There are many who are arrested in bunches, two or three together, and as they leave it's hard to know how they are connected to the men around – whether they are all one stable or couples of individual pimps and whores. These are the two occasions when the prostitutes I see are open and jovial – paying their fines or waiting in the pens. Then they seem together, giggling about the whole thing, walking around together. There is something about the way they relate to each other that I haven't seen among women in a long time, not since I was a child. It's a wild, silly kind of camaraderie. But I cannot trust it much: the best-friend routine, the effusiveness of our childhood, girlhood chumming was pretty phony. This has the same quality for me, the same nervous superficiality, the same illusory solidarity – longed for and impossible, therefore counterfeited, parodied. I cannot believe in the reality of this intimacy because I know that many of the women talking to each other, seemingly such good buddies, don't even know each other. Except that they've seen each other in the pens often, maybe spent time in the House of Detention together, or just seen each other around the court a lot. But in their lives, this is probably one of the few ways in which they enjoy the company of other women – the rest of the time isolated from each other by the pimps and the johns.

It is only in the pens that I can get attention or response from the women I try to work with; in court all their attention is riveted on the men. In court they are uninterested in me because I am a woman, and therefore, by definition, powerless. It's not a put down, not hostility, only their conviction that my sex makes me impotent to help them and they must relate to those in power over them. Then too, the only image of 'straight' women they have, of non-prostitutes, is one of contemptuous, moralistic, jealous, or disapproving respectable women. So there is little to encourage them to speak with me. But in the pens it is possible to relate to them somewhat, to interview them, to try to help.

I never use the phrase 'women's liberation'. I did once or twice early on and people sort of nodded unresponsively. So I gave that up. What I do now is simply tell the women why I'm talking to them, and sometimes they may end up mentioning women's lib. But I don't start off announcing I'm in women's lib and trying to relate to you because I think you're my sister. What I try to do is come on as straight, as direct, and as open as I can, and not go through any legal junk, but just begin to talk to them about their lives, what they've done, when they were married, when they've had kids and where their kids are, how long they've been in the House of Detention, and what they've been picked up for before. It's very rare, in fact it only happened twice, that a woman began to talk to me without my asking, really began to talk to me about her feelings about it all. Generally, when I've talked to them awhile, they do become responsive. But then, you know, considering all the thousands of women who go through these pens, I really haven't talked to that many. What I have done more than others is to see and carefully observe the way that they are treated here. But the feeling of distance is so enormous, the conditions themselves so impossible, you feel un-comfortable – you do not really have an opportunity to talk. You can't really talk to somebody when you're in front and they're behind bars. Even if you can come on in a way that will open them up, you can't talk to somebody about that kind of stuff if the situation is one where they're the ones that are getting fucked over and you're not. Immediately there is an inequality very hard to bridge. The only women I've talked to who had been in prostitution and who were interested and really cared about women's liberation were the women at Phoenix House, the drug rehabilitation centre. Elsewhere, what happens is that we talk of things that concern women, things women undergo, and strong feelings of sisterhood, closeness, concern, and strength just come out – not couched in the terms and jargon of the movement – but spontaneously emerging out of this shared experience. There is a communion of emotion, even if at this point politicized discussions of it only inter-fere.

*

Prostitution arrests vary enormously from day to day: one day thirty-five arrests for prostitution and none for drugs; the next day only ten prostitution arrests and fifteen for drugs. You really get the feeling that when the police do go out, they do a whole armful, probably because somebody called up and said, 'West Forty-fourth Street is bothering me, would you go over and clean it up.' The cops delicately refer to the vice squad, the plain clothes unit that does all the prostitution arrests, as the Pussy Brigade. And that's just the way they see it; it's just picking up the cunt, bringing it in, and letting it go loose again. Obviously, there's a lot of graft going on, a lot of give and take between the women and the cops; they've known each other for a long time and they're known to watch out for each other. There's not even the semblance of hostility between them. In fact, there may be something quite opposite, a total passivity on the part of the woman in relation to the police, but there is also a whole lot of what sociologists call 'accommodating' behaviour too. The scene in court is astonishing: the woman is absolutely flirting throughout the whole proceedings. She's doing it when she comes in; she does it when she's going out with the cops and clerks. It doesn't break down for a minute. That interchange is very weird to watch, and it's something that would take a long time to explain, but you know the woman's security and advantage lie in maintaining this relationship.

There was a woman who came in Tuesday, and like most of the women who came in she wore a wig (a trivial item but I find it significant, basic to the whole sense of remoteness, of self-distancing that goes on, the escapism). This woman was truly beautiful, with a really beautiful face, a black woman, wearing an enormous blond wig, a halter top with lots of empty space around the belly-button, with a high chest and wearing a very short skirt. From what I could tell (and I tried to watch her closely during the twenty-five minutes she was there rapping with everyone) she seemed to be enormously attached to the cop who had arrested her. She was flirting with him, even trying to talk to him, but not in the usual manner, that casual back and forth I hear every day: 'Hey, Tina, glad to see you again. What's it this time, baby? Sure. See you around.' This time it seemed different. She really cared: she looked sorry to leave. She kept on looking back at him – and that tore me up.

Ultimately I have come to understand the legal treatment of prostitution is only a farce. The court is merely a machine, processing an average of thirty women a day on loitering and prostitution charges, spitting out people like paper wads. The women I saw while doing statistical work in the court clerk's office, arraignment section, are very different from the group below in the pens, if only because they are sufficiently well off to get bailed out. Such women are not the committed cases, not the addicts, not the petty thieves. The rest down below stairs I remember most as being totally drugged out, their passivity a wall between us, between themselves and the world. But the group who come to court after bail, dressed up and eager to deal their way out of charges, look well kept and they usually show up with this unctuous lawyer, who's really a pig. What takes place in court is just the machine part of it, the racket part of it, how it actually works, coming in and going out. And it's nothing. Just like going to the doctor. Just as quick and just as routine.

The real reasons why the law was changed and the prostitution charge raised to a misdemeanour have obviously nothing to do with the stated intention given out at the time, namely the need for longer periods of rehabilitation, but only reflect the varying pressure the city feels from businessmen to clean up hotels. This is also the major block to legalization.

Since no one takes it seriously the entire legal aspect of prostitution is just bullshit, based on nothing but some kind of out-of-nowhere sense that they just must get this show into production over and over again, not because it matters or because it'll change anything or because anyone believes there is anything wrong with it at all – but because it is essential to keep up appearances. It's clear that prostitutes are the greatest spectacle in the court, every day's choicest entertainment. What happens to them matters to no one. They're no threat, but the law keeps on picking them up. They have relationships with the cops, and the judges know them too; the whole system bleeds them sexually and economically. They put out and they pay their fines. Public decorum is satisfied because whores are arrested. This is the justice men bestow on women.

SOCIOLOGY

BLACK SKIN WHITE MASKS Frantz Fanon 50p
The experience of a black man in a white world: A
psychological and philosophical analysis of the state of being a
negro. Fanon portrays the negro face to face with his race, the fact
of blackness, and the absurdity of his enslavement.

CONSCIOUSNESS AND SOCIETY H. Stuart Hughes 75p
The re-orientation of European social thought from 1890–1930;
the ideas and works of Freud, Croce, Bergson, Jung, Sorel,
Weber, Durkheim, Proust, Mann, Gide, Hesse, etc.

CRIME AND PERSONALITY H. J. Eysenck 60p
Are criminals born or made? Professor Eysenck examines how
heredity can determine personality differences and how 'conscience'
can act on the individual. A corrective to environmental analyses
of the cause of crime.

THE DIALECTIC OF SEX Shulamith Firestone 50p
The most articulate modern spokesman for the Radical Feminists
goes beyond Marx and Engels to find the source of all exploitative
systems in the biological/cultural relationship between the sexes—
and presents a blueprint for the first fully successful revolution in
history.

THE DRUGTAKERS Jock Young 60p
Jock Young explores in detail the nature, extent and origins of
international drug use today and shows that it is not drugs but sub-
cultures that are condemned.

*All these books are available at your local bookshop or newsagent; or can be
ordered direct from the publisher. Just tick the titles you want and fill in the
form below.*

Name ....

Address ....

....

Write to Paladin Cash Sales, P.O. Box 11, Falmouth, Cornwall TR10
9EN. Please enclose remittance to the value of the cover price plus 10p
postage and packing for one book, 5p for each additional copy. *Granada
Publishing reserve the right to show new retail prices on covers, which may
differ from those previously advertised in the text or elsewhere.*